CD-ROM

FACT*finders*

INTERACTIVE MULTIMEDIA

OUTER SPACE

Written by
Harry Ford and Kay Barnham

Designed by
Chris Leishman

Illustrated by
Arcana Studios and Peter Bull

McGraw-Hill Consumer Products

Harry Ford is a lecturer at the Caird
Planetarium, the Old Royal Observatory,
National Maritime Museum, where he
regularly answers children's questions.
Formerly curator of the Mills Observatory,
Dundee, Scotland, he and his wife Lynne
built the planetarium at the Central Museum,
Southend. In 1985, he was awarded the
Lorimer Gold Medal of the Astronomical
Society of Edinburgh, Scotland.

ZIGZAG PUBLISHING

This edition published in 1998 by SMITHMARK
Publishers, a division of U.S. Media Holdings, Inc.,
115 West 18th Street, New York, NY 10011

Produced by: ZigZag, an imprint of Quadrillion Publishing
Ltd., Godalming, Surrey, England, GU7 1XW

Editors: Kay Barnham and Hazel Songhurst
Managing Editor: Nicola Wright
Design Manager: Kate Buxton
Production: Zoe Fawcett
Additional Illustrations by: Derek Bishop and Guy Smith
Cover illustration: Derek Bishop
Series concept: Tony Potter

Color separations: RCS Graphics Ltd, Leeds, England
Printed in Singapore

Distributed in the U.S. by
McGRAW-HILL CONSUMER PRODUCTS,
A Division of The McGraw-Hill Companies,
8787 Orion Place, Columbus, OH 43240

ISBN 1-57768-764-7

1 2 3 4 5 6 7 8 9 10 QUAD 04 03 02 01 00 99

Contents

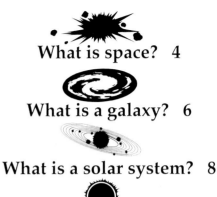

This book answers all your questions about space and spaceflight. It is packed with amazing facts about planets, solar systems, galaxies and the spacecraft we use to explore the Universe!

Have you ever wondered what planets are made of or why stars twinkle? How do astronauts train and where are spacecraft built? These questions and many more are answered by our space expert.

You can also discover how to become an astronaut and where to find out more information about space.

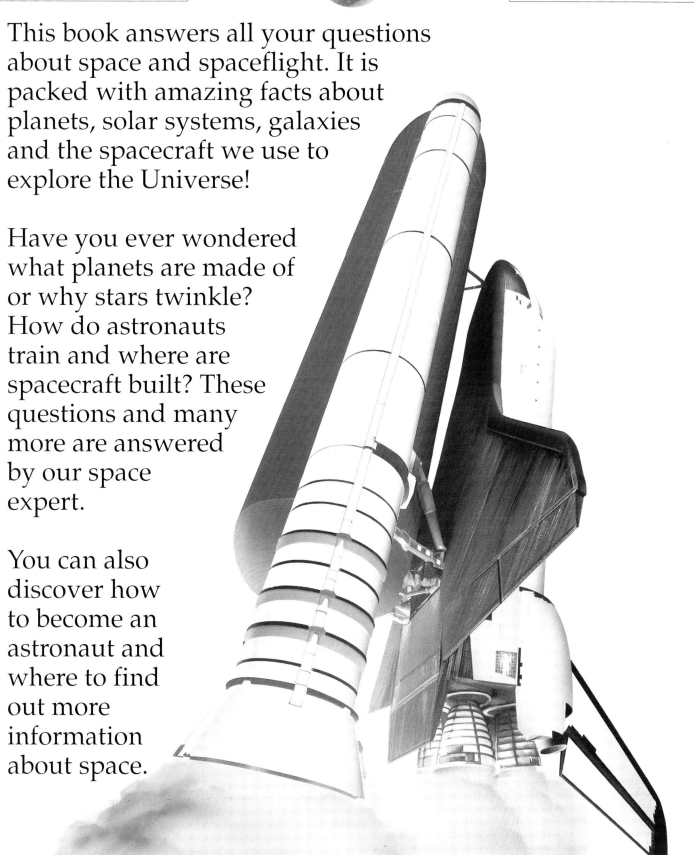

Scientists think that the Universe may contain huge amounts of invisible material called dark matter.

What is space?

Space is the name we give to the region beyond our planet, Earth, which may stretch on forever. Space is made of nothing at all, but it has lots of things in it, such as planets and stars. Space and its contents are called the Universe.

Q How was the Universe made?

A Many scientists believe that the Universe is the result of an explosion called the Big Bang, which occurred about 14 billion years ago.

Q What was the Big Bang?

A The Big Bang was an explosion of all the matter in the Universe, which was squashed into a tiny area at more than 27 billion°F. The matter exploded so quickly that, within a hundredth of a second, the Universe was as big as the Sun! It continued to grow.

Q Is there anything left of the Big Bang?

A Scientists have found that the average temperature of the Universe is 8°F above absolute zero, which is the coldest temperature possible. This heat could come from the Big Bang continuing to slow down.

Absolute zero

Q Is the Universe still getting bigger?

A Yes. Scientists have discovered that matter and groups of stars are still moving further away from each other. However, they are now moving much more slowly than just after the Big Bang.

In 1929, Edwin Hubble discovered that the Universe was getting bigger. This led to the Big Bang theory.

Stars would explode if gravity were not holding their material together.

Q How do we measure large distances in space?

A Other stars and planets are so far away that if we measured the distance in miles, the number would be enormous. Instead, scientists measure these huge distances in light-years. Light travels at 186,000 mi. per second, so a light-year is the distance light travels in one year - 5,878,000,000,000 mi.!

Q What is the Universe made of?

A Everything in the Universe is made of atoms.When the Universe had cooled down after the Big Bang, tiny particles called protons, electrons and neutrons formed. These particles joined together in different ways to make up different sorts of atoms. For example, a helium atom is made up of two electrons, two protons and two neutrons.

Q How were stars and planets formed?

A Atoms have gravity, which means that they pull things toward them. After the Big Bang, gravity made atoms clump together to form stars and planets. Stars are made of hydrogen and helium atoms. Solid planets are made of carbon and iron atoms.

Q How big is the Universe?

A Scientists do not know how big the Universe is. So far, their instruments have been able to see as far as 300 million light-years into space, where there is a long line of galaxies. (A galaxy is a group of stars.) Scientists do not yet know what is beyond!

What is a galaxy?

A galaxy is a group of millions of stars. A spiral galaxy looks like a huge, spinning Catherine wheel. Most of the stars are in the centre, with trailing spiral arms of stars around the outside.

Q What is the Milky Way?

A The Milky Way is the name of our galaxy. It is a spiral galaxy and our Solar System is in one of its spiral arms. The centre of the Milky Way can sometimes be spotted at night. It looks like a misty streak across the sky.

Q How many galaxies are there in the Universe?

A There may be 100 billion galaxies!

Q Which is the biggest galaxy?

A The Andromeda Galaxy is the biggest galaxy of those near the Milky Way. On a clear night, all you can see of this galaxy is a small fuzzy blob, but it has twice as many stars as the Milky Way - perhaps as many as 200 billion! There may be galaxies even bigger than Andromeda.

Q When were galaxies discovered?

A The first astronomers called misty patches in the sky nebulae, which means mist. It was not until early this century that it was found that many of these mysterious nebulae were actually distant galaxies.

The Milky Way measures about 588,000,000,000,000,000 mi., or 100,000 light years across.

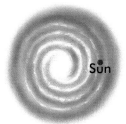
Sun

The ancient Greeks gave the Milky Way its name because they thought it was made of drops of milk from the breasts of the goddess Hera.

The Milky Way measures about 588,000,000,000,000,000 mi., or 100,000 light years across.

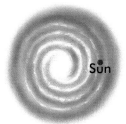
Sun

The ancient Greeks gave the Milky Way its name because they thought it was made of drops of milk from the breasts of the goddess Hera.

Q **What is at the centre of the Milky Way?**

A Scientists have discovered that there is a huge amount of hot gas at the centre of our galaxy. Some experts think that this may be caused by a enormous, swirling black hole which is slowly sucking in dust, gas and even light. You can find out more about black holes on page 175.

There are millions of spiral galaxies in the Universe. These galaxies contain many young stars.

Q **Are galaxies evenly spread throughout space?**

A There are enormous distances between galaxies, but scientists think that they are grouped in clusters. There may be thousands of galaxies in each cluster. Clusters of galaxies may, in turn, be grouped in superclusters.

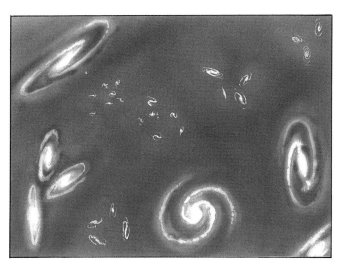

Q **Are all galaxies shaped like the Milky Way?**

A No. Galaxies can also be shaped like barred spirals and ellipses. Other galaxies have no definite shape.

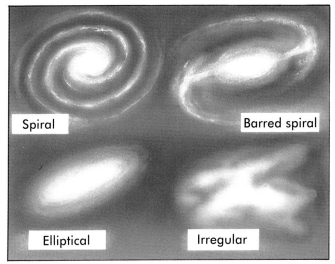
Spiral
Barred spiral
Elliptical
Irregular

You can find out more about black holes on page 175.

What is a solar system?

A solar system is a group of planets and moons which travel around, or orbit, a star. Every star is actually a sun, which may have its own solar system.

Q What are the planets in our Solar System called?

A The nine planets which orbit our Sun are called Mercury, Venus, Earth, Mars, Jupiter, Saturn, Uranus, Neptune and Pluto.

Q How old is the Solar System?

A Our Solar System was formed about 4.6 billion years ago, nearly 10 billion years after the Universe began. New stars and solar systems are still being formed!

Q How long does it take each planet to orbit the Sun?

A It takes Earth a year to travel once around the Sun. Planets nearer the Sun take less time and planets further away take longer. The table below shows how long it takes each planet to orbit the Sun.

Q Can we see any planets from Earth without a telescope?

A The five planets nearest to Earth can be seen with the naked eye. These are Mercury, Venus, Mars, Jupiter and Saturn. They were first sighted in prehistoric times.

Saturn

Mercury	87.97	days
Venus	224.70	days
Earth	365.26	days
Mars	686.98	days
Jupiter	11.86	years
Saturn	29.50	years
Uranus	84.01	years
Neptune	164.79	years
Pluto	248.54	years

Uranus

Neptune

Pluto

Ganymede is the biggest moon in our Solar System. It measures 3,268 mi. across and orbits Jupiter.

The planets in our Solar System are named after the Roman gods. Mars was the god of war.

Q What is the difference between a planet and a moon?

A Planets orbit suns, while moons orbit planets.

Q Are there any other planets in our Solar System beyond Pluto?

A So far, six tiny planets have been found. The first two have been named Smiley and Karla. Scientists once hoped that a large planet would be discovered, but now it seems unlikely.

Q Do other planets have moons?

A Yes. Most planets have moons. Saturn has 19 moons, Jupiter and Uranus have 16 each, Neptune has 6, Mars has 2 and Pluto has only 1 moon.

Here you can see the Sun and planets in our Solar System (not to scale).

Mars

Earth

Venus

Mercury

Jupiter

Sun

What is the Sun?

Before clocks were invented, people used sundials to tell what time of day it was.

The Sun is a star. It is a great, glowing ball of hydrogen and helium gas. Without the Sun's light and heat, nothing could survive on Earth.

Q How hot is the Sun?

A The Sun is very hot indeed! Its surface is 16,394°F, and the temperature at the center measures 38 million°F!

Sunspots are cooler areas on the Sun's surface. Some are bigger than Earth.

Q Is Earth bigger than the Sun?

A No. Although, the Sun looks quite small to us, it is actually one million times bigger than our planet, Earth.

Earth ← The Sun is 92,961,000 mi. from Earth. → Sun

Q How do the Sun's rays affect Earth?

A Without the Sun's rays, life on Earth would die. Plants need the Sun's light to change carbon dioxide and water into the food they need. In turn, humans and animals rely on plants for their food supply.

This is a close-up view of the Sun.

A white dwarf star is a star that has used up its hydrogen fuel.

White dwarf

You must NEVER use a telescope or binoculars to look directly at the Sun - its light could blind you.

Q Will the Sun last for ever?

A It will last for many millions of years! In about 5 billion years' time, the Sun will have burnt up all of its hydrogen fuel. It will become a hundred times as bright as it is now, and swell up to swallow the nearest planets, including Earth. After another 100 million years, the Sun will shrink to become a white dwarf star.

Solar flares are huge clouds of glowing gases which loop above the Sun's surface.

Helios 2

Q Is the Sun moving?

A Yes. All the planets in our Solar System orbit the Sun and, in turn, our Solar System orbits the center of our galaxy, the Milky Way. It takes about 225 million years, or one cosmic year, for the Sun and nine planets to travel around the Milky Way once.

The Sun in the Milky Way (not to scale)

Q Can the Sun's rays be harmful?

A We receive the Sun's light and heat, but most of the dangerous rays, such as ultra violet rays, are stopped by the layers of gas in Earth's atmosphere. However, the ozone layer is getting thinner. Scientists believe that it is being damaged by chemicals from Earth.

The ozone layer

Q Can spacecraft get close to the Sun?

A The Sun is so hot that spacecraft cannot fly very near it. In 1976 *Helios 2* traveled to within 28,000,000 mi. of the Sun. This is closer than the Sun's nearest planet, Mercury.

Venus is always surrounded by clouds of sulphuric acid.

What are planets made of?

Venus

Like Earth, most of the smaller planets in our Solar System have a solid surface made of rock. However, the four biggest planets (Jupiter, Saturn, Uranus and Neptune) are made of gases!

Q Could we breathe on any other planet in our Solar System?

A No. One of Saturn's moons, Titan, may have an atmosphere made of nitrogen gas (which makes up four-fifths of Earth's atmosphere). However, to stay alive, human beings also need oxygen.

Q Is there life on other planets?

A All of the planets in the Solar System have been explored, using telescopes and space probes. So far, nothing living has been found. The other planets in our system all seem to be too hot, too cold, or made entirely of gases.

Q Are there mountains, valleys and volcanoes on other planets?

A Yes, most solid planets have geographical features like Earth. Scientists have found deserts, polar areas, mountains and valleys on Mars. Volcanoes have been found on Venus, Mars and Io (one of Jupiter's moons). The biggest volcano of all is on Mars. It is called Mount Olympus and it is 15 mi. high!

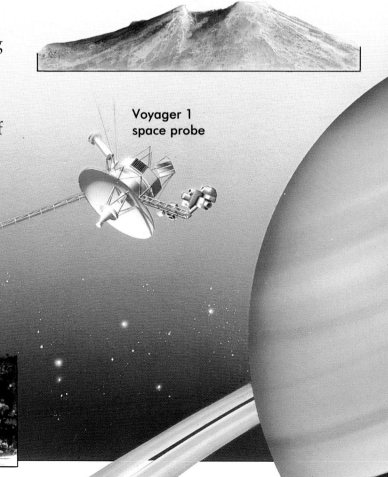

Voyager 1 space probe

Telescope

Space observatory

The Great Red Spot on Jupiter's surface is actually a furious storm.

Saturn's rings can be spotted even with a small telescope.

Q Why is Mars red?

A Mars is red because it is rusty! The surface of the planet is covered in iron oxide, or rust, which forms when iron mixes with small amounts of oxygen and water.

Q Why does Saturn have stripes?

A Saturn's atmosphere is made of different gases. Some of these gases do not mix and when Saturn spins, high winds blow the gas around the planet into stripes. Each stripe is a different mixture of gas.

Q What shape are planets?

A A planet may look round, but it is are shaped like an ellipse. This means that it looks like a squashed ball. Saturn and Jupiter spin very quickly so they are the most squashed planets.

Saturn's rings

Saturn

Q What are Saturn's rings made of?

A Saturn's rings are made of millions of particles of dust and ice. There are so many of them in orbit around Saturn that it makes the rings look solid. The rings shine because the ice particles in them reflect light.

Could people live on the Moon?

An astronaut last walked on the Moon in 1973.

There is no atmosphere on the Moon, so you would not be able to breathe. It is possible to set up scientific bases there, but anyone walking around on the Moon would need a space suit.

Q Why is the Moon covered in craters?

A Most of the Moon's craters were caused about three billion years ago by meteorites. These lumps of rock and iron hurled through Space and crashed into the Moon at high speed.

Q What are the dark areas on the Moon?

A When people first looked through telescopes at the Moon, they thought that the dark areas were seas. They gave them names, such as the Sea of Tranquility. It was later discovered that these seas were really areas of dry, dark lava from volcanic eruptions.

Q Why isn't Earth covered with craters ?

A Earth was once covered with craters, but most have been worn away by rain, wind and movement of the Earth's crust. There is no weather on the Moon, so its craters have not been worn away.

The Moon is bigger than the planet Pluto.

Pluto

Moon

The Moon is about 238,866 mi. from Earth. It would take you more than 9 years to walk there!

Q What is an eclipse of the Sun?

A This occurs when the Moon is directly between Earth and the Sun. For a few moments, the Sun's light is blocked and the Moon casts a shadow onto Earth, turning day into night!

An eclipse of the Sun

Q What happens when there is an eclipse of the Moon?

A This occurs when Earth is directly between the Moon and the Sun. We can only see the Moon because it reflects the Sun's light. If Earth travels between the Sun and the Moon, it stops the Sun's light from reaching the Moon, so the Moon seems to disappear.

Q Why does the Moon seem to change shape?

A The Sun's light only falls on one side of the Moon. It takes 27.3 days or one lunar month, for the Moon to orbit Earth. As the Moon orbits Earth, we see different amounts of the sunlit side of the Moon. When we can see all of the sunlit side, there is a full moon.

Last quarter

Full moon

New moon

First quarter

Q Does the Moon affect Earth?

A Yes, the Moon has its own gravity, which pulls Earth's seas toward it, making them bulge. As the Earth spins, the bulge moves around its surface. When the Moon is overhead, the sea reaches its highest level. When the Moon is over the coast, there is a high tide.

The Sun's gravity also has a small effect on Earth's seas. When the Sun and Moon both pull at once, there is a very high tide. This is called a spring tide.

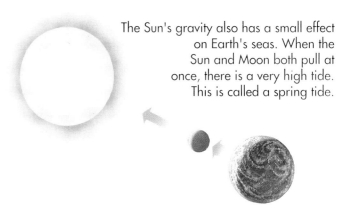

The word comet means "hairy star."

What is an asteroid belt?

There are thousands of pieces of rock, called asteroids, in orbit around the Sun. Most of these asteroids are grouped together between Mars and Jupiter. These large groups of rocks are known as asteroid belts.

Q What are comets made of?

A Comets are huge balls of shining, frozen rock, gas and dust. The comet has a tail made of gas and dust which blows out from it in the solar wind sent out by the Sun. There may be as many as 100 billion comets orbiting the Sun.

Q How big are comets?

A The Giotto Space Probe showed that the head of Halley's Comet was as large as a mountain. A comet's tail can be over 62 million mi. long!

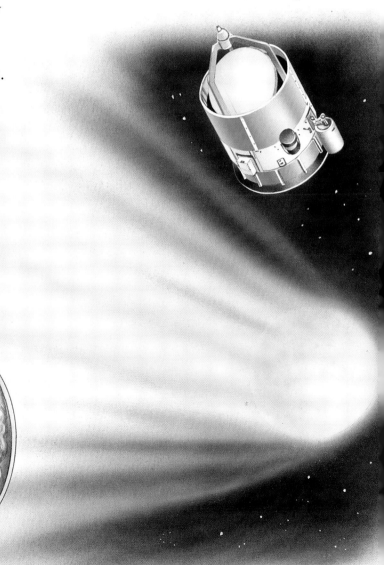

Q How did Halley's Comet get its name?

A In the 1600s, the brilliant scientist Edmond Halley realized that one particular comet orbited the Sun every 76 years. He correctly predicted that its next appearance would be in 1758. It will next be seen in 2062.

When lots of dust hits Earth's atmosphere, it burns up, and looks like lots of shooting stars. This is called a meteor shower.

A meteorite is a meteor that has fallen to Earth.

Q Did an asteroid kill the last of the dinosaurs?

A Perhaps. An asteroid which might have been as large as 6 mi. across fell near Yucatan, in Mexico, about 65 million years ago. The Chicxlub Crater made by this asteroid is 112 mi. across. The force of the blast caused tidal waves and earthquakes and threw huge clouds of dust into the sky. Scientists think that all land animals that weighed over 66 lbs. died, including the last of the dinosaurs.

Q What are shooting stars?

A Shooting stars are not stars at all! They are actually tiny pieces of dust, called meteors. When a comet flies past, dust from its burning tail falls toward Earth. When these particles of dust hit Earth's atmosphere at very high speed, they burn up. On Earth, this looks as if a star is falling from the sky.

Q Which is the biggest asteroid in our solar system?

A Asteroids are bigger than meteors and are like small planets. The largest asteroid in our Solar System is Ceres, which is over 621 mi. wide.

The force of the meteorite explosion in Siberia created such strong winds, that a farmer 124 mi. away was almost blown over.

Q When was the last time a large meteor hit Earth?

A The last time this happened was in 1908 in a remote area of Siberia, Russia. Great areas of trees were knocked down by the blast.

The nearest star to our Sun is Proxima Centauri, which is 4.3 light-years or 25,277 billion mi. away.

Stars twinkle because the light they send toward Earth is bent by air currents moving around in our atmosphere. If you were to travel above Earth's atmosphere, the stars would not twinkle at all!

Q Why do stars shine?

A Stars shine because they are hot, just like our Sun. Inside a star, hydrogen gas turns into helium gas, which gives out energy in the form of light, heat and other invisible rays.

Q Can we tell the time by the stars?

A Yes. Earth spins around once every 24 hours. During the night, stars appears to move across the sky. It is possible to tell the time when their changing positions are measured. Before clocks, stars were an important way of telling the time at night.

Q Where is the best place to see stars?

A Bright stars can be seen easily from anywhere on clear nights, but the best place to see the dimmer stars is in the countryside. In towns, artificial light from street lighting fills the sky, making it difficult to see the dimmer stars.

The Sun is so far away that its light takes 8 minutes to reach us on Earth.

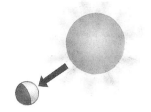

A star is formed in our galaxy every 18 days. That means there are 20 new stars each year!

Q What is the best time of night to see stars?

A The best time to see stars is when the sky is at its darkest. This is at midnight, when the Sun is on the opposite side of Earth.

Q Can we measure a star's brightness?

A Yes. A star's brightness is called its magnitude. A star of magnitude 0 is very bright. Stars of magnitude 5 are only just visible. Really bright stars have minus magnitudes. Sirius, the brightest star in the sky, has a magnitude of -1.5.

Q How did sailors use the stars to find their way at night ?

A If you live in the northern hemisphere, one star seems to stay still. This is called the Pole Star as it is almost directly over the North Pole. Sailors knew that its position showed the north, so they could then work out in which direction to sail.

Q Can we see the same stars throughout the year?

A No. Earth is orbiting the Sun, so during the year we get to see the stars all around the Sun. The Pole Star is almost directly over our Solar System, so people living in the northern hemisphere can see it all year round. For people who live in the southern hemisphere, the same is true of the Southern Cross Star.

Sun

How are stars formed?

The Sun is a yellow star. Its surface temperature is 16,394°F.

Stars form when hydrogen atoms in space are attracted to each other and clump together. The gas begins to burn and the star shines.

Q How long do stars last?

A The larger a star is, the shorter its life will be. Our Sun is quite small compared with some stars and has a life-span of 10 billion years. Really large stars only last for a few million years.

Q Are stars the same color?

A No. If you look closely at stars, they are different colors. A star's color depends on its temperature. Blue stars are the hottest. Red stars are cooler. Here are some stars and their approximate surface temperatures:

●	Red	up to 11,000°F
●	Orange	about 14,000°F
○	Yellow	15,000 - 21,000°F
○	White	21,000 - 27,000°F
○	Blue-white	27,000 - 54,000°F
○	Blue	54,000 - 135,000°F

Q What is a supernova?

A A supernova is a huge star which has blown up after running out of fuel. After it explodes, the star collapses and debris is flung into space to form new stars and planets. All that is left of the supernova is a small neutron star.

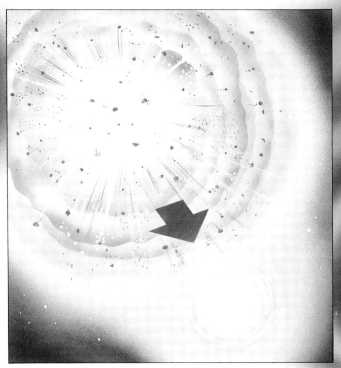

Q What is a pulsar?

A A pulsar is a spinning neutron star, left behind after a large supernova explosion. It is called a pulsar because of the pulses, or flashes of energy, it sends out as it spins.

Some nebulae are made from debris left behind after supernovae have exploded (right).

Red stars are the dimmest. They are the most difficult to see.

Q **What is a black hole?**

A When a really large star explodes into a supernovae, a strange thing happens. The star collapses so much that all of the material in it is squashed together. This squashed star has so much gravity that it attracts other material, even light, toward it and sucks it all in, so that it can never escape. This is called a black hole.

Black hole

Q **What is a white dwarf star?**

A At the end of their lifetimes, some smaller stars become very big and bright, before shrinking into white dwarf stars. Eventually, these white dwarf stars cool down and fade away.

Q **What are quasars?**

A Quasars are tiny star-like objects far away in space. We can only see them because they give out so much energy. Astronomers are still not sure exactly what they are!

Q **What are wandering stars?**

A Wandering stars are actually planets. We can see five planets - Mercury, Venus, Mars, Jupiter and Saturn - from Earth without a telescope. These planets look as if they are wandering around in the sky.

A planisphere is a star chart you adjust to show which stars are in the sky on any night of the year.

What is a constellation?

Planisphere

A constellation is a pattern of stars. Ancient astronomers found that constellations were easier to recognize than individual stars. These constellations were given names.

Sagittarius
Capricornus
Aquarius
Scorpius
Pisces
Libra
Aries
Virgo
Taurus
Leo
Gemini
Cancer

These twelve constellations are called the signs of the zodiac. Here you can see their names and the people, animals or objects they represent.

Q What are the signs of the zodiac?

A The Earth orbits the Sun each year, so we see different constellations at different times of the year. During the year, we pass twelve important constellations. These are called the signs of the zodiac. Zodiac means 'circle of animals', because most of the signs are of animals.

Q Who named the stars and constellations?

A Early civilizations such as the Greeks and Romans, named the stars and constellations. We still use many of the same names today, some of which are more than 4,000 years old.

Q Do constellations change shape?

A Yes. It takes millions of years for Earth to orbit the center of the Milky Way. As our planet travels through space, we slowly get a different view of the stars. About 100,000 years ago, the Big Dipper constellation looked quite a different shape.

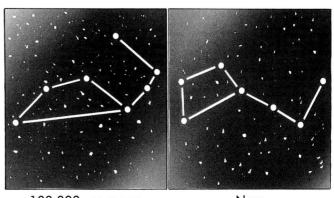

100,000 years ago   Now

There are 88 constellations which can be seen during the year in different parts of the world.

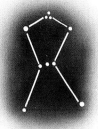

The constellation called Orion can be seen from both the northern and the southern hemisphere.

Q What is astrology?

A Astrology claims to predict the future using the positions of the planets. Astrologers believe that the planets may signal good or bad luck as they move into each sign of the zodiac.

Here, Venus is in the Scorpio constellation.

Q What is a planetarium?

A A planetarium is a place where you can see stars and planets projected onto the inside of a large dome. A lecturer can show you the stars' positions during the night and throughout the year. When you visit a planetarium, it is just like watching the night sky without having to sit outside!

Planetarium

Q Are the stars in each constellation the same distance from Earth?

A No. The stars in a constellation may look as if they are all the same distance from Earth. Some may be only a few light years away, while others may be hundreds or even thousands of light years away.

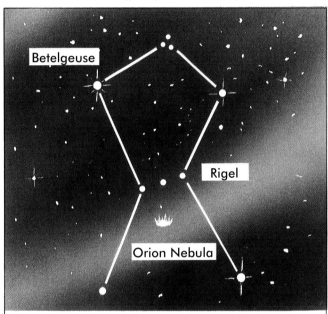

Betelgeuse

Rigel

Orion Nebula

These stars in the Orion constellation are all different distances from Earth:

Betelgeuse	586 light years away
Rigel	880 light years away
Orion nebula	1600 light years away

Q Is astrology the same all over the world?

A No. Instead of using the positions of the planets to make predictions, Oriental or Chinese astrology looks at how often eclipses, comets, shooting stars and supernovae occur.

Two astronomers used Newton's laws to predict the existence of Neptune. They were proven right when it was later seen in 1846.

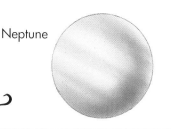

Neptune

Who were the first astronomers?

The Ancient Greeks were the first scientific astronomers. They worked out the size of Earth and that there were enormous distances between our Sun and other stars.

Q When were telescopes invented?

A Telescopes were invented at the end of the 1500s. Galileo Galilei, an Italian astronomer, was the first to use a telescope to look at the night sky. At that time, many people believed that the Sun orbited Earth. Galileo was condemned by the church for saying that the Sun, not Earth, was the center of the Solar System. He was, of course, correct!

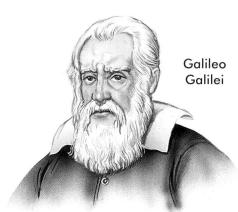

Galileo Galilei

Q What is a radio telescope?

A Some objects cannot be seen with an optical telescope, but the radio waves that they give out can be detected with a radio telescope. Karl Jansky built the first radio telescope in 1932.

Radio telescope

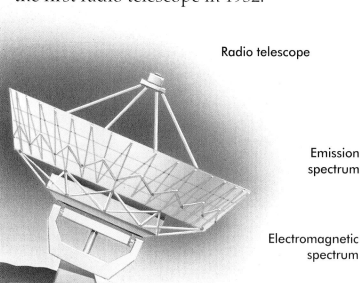

Q What is the electromagnetic spectrum?

A The electromagnetic spectrum is the range of all the energy we know about in the Universe. It stretches from wide radio waves to narrow gamma rays. Stars give out different amounts of each type of energy. This information can be recorded as a sort of bar code, called an emission spectrum. Scientists use this information to find out what materials a star is made of.

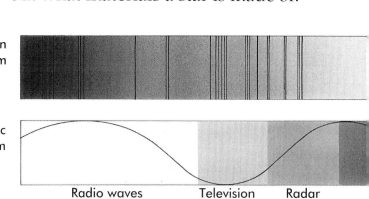

Emission spectrum

Electromagnetic spectrum

Radio waves   Television waves   Radar waves

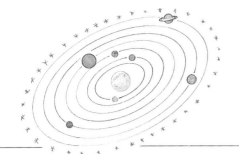

Ptolemy was a famous early astronomer who worked in Egypt. He thought that the Sun, the Moon, planets and stars in our Solar System orbited Earth.

Q How does a refractor telescope work?

A A refractor telescope uses a curved lens to bend and magnify light from distant objects, such as stars.

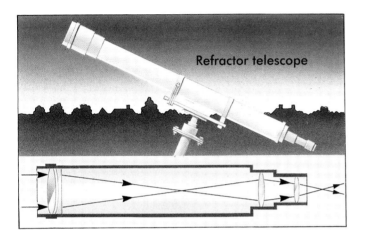

Refractor telescope

Q How does a reflector telescope work?

A This telescope bends light with mirrors. It was invented by scientist Isaac Newton in 1668.

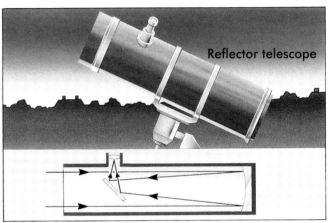

Reflector telescope

Q Which is the most powerful optical telescope in the world?

A This is a reflecting telescope with a mirror that measures 19 ft. across. It weighs 78 tons and is housed at the Zlenchukskya Observatory in the Russian Caucasus Mountains. The Keck telescope in Hawaii is bigger, but this is made up of several hexagonal mirrors joined together like a honeycomb.

If a color appears on a star's emission spectrum, that star is giving out a particular type of energy. Black lines show that some types of energy are missing.

Q Who discovered gravity?

A Sir Isaac Newton discovered the force of gravity in 1665. Gravity is a pulling force that keeps the stars and planets in their orbits. Earth's gravity stops the Moon from floating away into space. The Sun's gravity keeps all the planets in our Solar System in orbit around it.

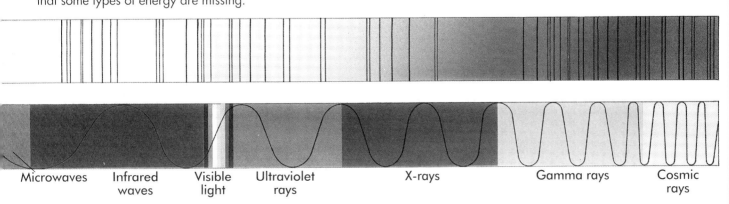

Microwaves Infrared waves Visible light Ultraviolet rays X-rays Gamma rays Cosmic rays

The Space Shuttle orbits Earth at 17,400 mph.

Earth's gravity is so strong that rockets are needed to propel satellites and other spacecraft out of the atmosphere and into space.

Q How does a rocket work?

A If a balloon is filled with air and then released, it speeds along - a rocket works in the same way. A mixture of hydrogen and oxygen fuel explodes all the time, pushing hot gas out of the back of the rocket and propelling it along.

Q What are satellites?

A Satellites are space vehicles which orbit our planet. They can relay television, radio and telephone signals around Earth. Some satellites give us weather forecasts, and others look for evidence of resources, such as oil, hidden beneath Earth's surface.

Q Which was the first satellite?

A The first satellite was *Sputnik 1*, launched in Russia on October 4, 1957. It stayed in orbit for only 90 days. The only equipment that it carried was a radio transmitter, so that scientists could track its position from Earth.

Sputnik 1

Q What happens to rockets after launching a spacecraft?

A Rockets are only needed for the first few seconds of a spacecraft's journey. They then fall back down to Earth, land in the sea and are recovered by special ships.

The fuel tank holds 1 million gallons of fuel to power the orbiter's own rockets.

The rocket boosters give the Shuttle extra push for the lift-off. They fall off only 30 seconds into the flight.

A spacecraft has to travel at 28,856 mph to escape Earth's atmosphere.

Some satellites always stay above the same part of Earth. These are usually weather satellites.

There are heat-resistant tiles on the Orbiter that stop it from bursting into flames when it re-enters Earth's atmosphere.

For the launch, the Orbiter is attached to the fuel tank and boosters for the launch. It needs no fuel to glide back to Earth after its mission.

The Orbiter's rockets give most of the power to push it out of Earth's atmosphere

Q **How do spacecraft land back on Earth safely?**

A Spacecraft such as *Apollo* and *Soyuz* both land in the sea when they come back to Earth. However, the Space Shuttle is specially designed to land like a normal airplane on a runway.

Q **Can spacecraft be reused?**

A Until 1981, all spacecraft were only used once, but new types of craft such as the American Space Shuttle and the Russian *Buran* Shuttle can be used over and over again.

Q **Where are spacecraft built?**

A American spacecraft, such as the Space Shuttle and *Saturn V*, are built in the largest scientific building in the world. This is the Vehicle Assembly Building (VAB) at the Kennedy Space Center in Florida. The VAB's doors are 460 ft. high, so spacecraft can be rolled out.

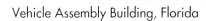

Vehicle Assembly Building, Florida

Russian astronauts are called cosmonauts.

Yuri Gagarin from Russia was the first man in space on April 12, 1961. In 1963, Valentina Tereshkova became the first woman to be launched into space.

Q How many astronauts have been to the Moon?

A A total of twelve astronauts have landed on the Moon in spacecraft called *Apollo 11, 12, 14, 15, 16* and *17*. Unfortunately, *Apollo 13* had many technical problems and its lunar module was unable to land. The crew had to fly the damaged spacecraft using the stars' positions as a guide. They landed safely back on Earth.

Q What is a space station?

A A space station is a large spacecraft which stays in orbit around Earth. Scientists can live and work there for long periods of time. The Russian *Mir* Space Station was launched in 1986.

Q What was the first living thing to go into space?

A A dog called Lemonchik (meaning "little lemon") was the first living being to go into space. It was launched on the *Sputnik 2* mission. Unfortunately, it died when the oxygen ran out.

Q How do astronauts train?

A Astronauts have special training to prepare them for the feeling of weightlessness in space. Before their flight, astronauts often rehearse space experiments and missions underwater. A swimming pool is filled with very salty water, which makes the astronauts float as if they were in space.

In space, weightlessness makes it very difficult to eat meals off plates. Instead, astronauts suck food out of tubes.

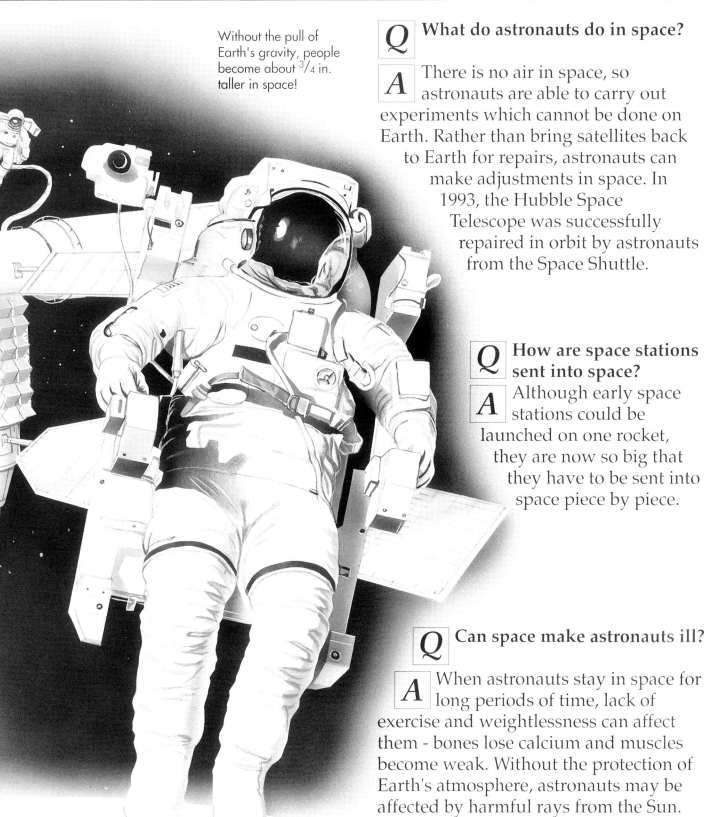

Without the pull of Earth's gravity, people become about $^3/_4$ in. taller in space!

Q **What do astronauts do in space?**

A There is no air in space, so astronauts are able to carry out experiments which cannot be done on Earth. Rather than bring satellites back to Earth for repairs, astronauts can make adjustments in space. In 1993, the Hubble Space Telescope was successfully repaired in orbit by astronauts from the Space Shuttle.

Q **How are space stations sent into space?**

A Although early space stations could be launched on one rocket, they are now so big that they have to be sent into space piece by piece.

Q **Can space make astronauts ill?**

A When astronauts stay in space for long periods of time, lack of exercise and weightlessness can affect them - bones lose calcium and muscles become weak. Without the protection of Earth's atmosphere, astronauts may be affected by harmful rays from the Sun.

The American space agency is called N.A.S.A. This stands for National Aeronautics and Space Administration.

How can you find out more?

Visiting a planetarium, joining an astronomy club or looking round a science museum are just a few of the ways you can find out more about space.

Q Are there plans for any more space stations?

A Yes. An American space station called "Freedom" is planned, but the enormous cost means that the project has been postponed several times. If *Freedom* ever does get off the ground, it will probably link up with the Russian *Mir* space station, allowing Russian and American astronauts to work together in space.

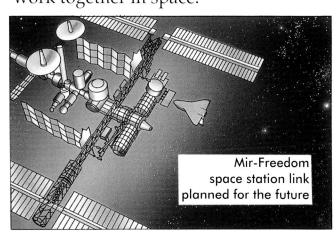

Mir-Freedom space station link planned for the future

Q How can we see further into space?

A Earth's atmosphere blocks out many of the rays which come from distant objects in the Universe. The Hubble Space Telescope was sent above the atmosphere so that scientists could have a clearer view and see further into space. Other instruments, such as radio telescopes, could also be sent into space to find out more about the Universe.

Q How far have spacecraft travelled into space?

A The *Pioneer 10* space probe has travelled the furthest distance. It flew past Pluto in 1986 and is still heading out into deep space!

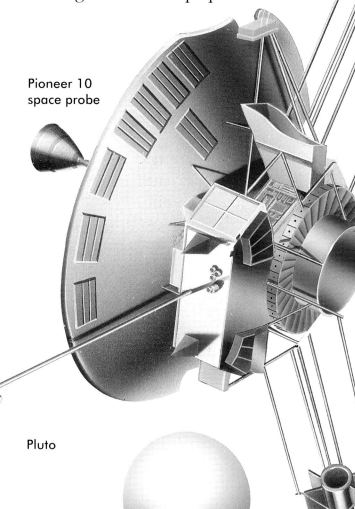

Pioneer 10 space probe

Pluto

Captain John Young has been into space more than anyone else. He has flown on 6 space flights.

One of the next planned space mission is a trip to Mars. N.A.S.A. hopes to send astronauts there in the next 50 years.

Q Have we received any messages from space?

A Not yet! Scientists have been listening for messages from space for years, but so far none have been received. As far as we know, signals can only be sent at the speed of light. If there were alien beings in other solar systems, they would be so far away that any messages we received from them would be thousands or even millions of years old by the time they reached us.

Q Can anyone be an astronaut?

A When space travel first began, astronauts were all specially trained airplane pilots. Now, however, astronauts can be experts from different sciences who are sent into space to carry out experiments. However, competition is so fierce that as well as being science experts, hopeful astronauts also have to be lucky enough to be chosen!

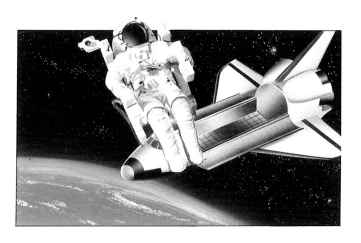

Q What messages have been sent to space?

A Yes, in 1977, two probes called *Pioneer 10* and *Pioneer 11* were launched into space. They each carried a plaque (see below) with information about our planet. Each plaque showed pictures of human beings and also space maps which gave directions to the Sun and showed the position of Earth in our Solar System.

Message on board Pioneer probes

Q How do you become an astronomer?

A Anyone can study the night sky! You can stargaze from your back garden and even a small telescope gives a better view of the stars. Astronomers usually study astronomy, mathematics, physics or another science at university, and work in observatories around the world as part of their training.

Index

Air War
Desert Storm

By Lou Drendel

squadron/signal publications

F-15s of the 27th Tactical Fighter Squadron, 1st Tactical Fighter Wing deployed from Langley Air Force Base, Virginia, to Saudi Arabia in some fourteen hours. The Eagles refueled at least eight times, usually from KC-10 Extenders. The Eagle was designed as a pure air superiority fighter and is a big aircraft, with a wingspan of forty-three feet and length of sixty-four feet. The F-15C has a maximum takeoff weight of 68,470 pounds.

Introduction

In all the debate over the conduct of the Vietnam War, a number of so-called "experts" repeatedly told us that Vietnam was proof ...once again...that airpower alone could not win a war. Bombing an enemy only hardens his will to resist. After the Vietnam War, these "experts" told us that the military budget was bloated by $600 toilet seats and $500 screwdrivers. They told us that "Star Wars" technology was at best "destabilizing" and at worst, money down the drain. They insisted that high tech weapons were too complex and they would not work in combat. They told us that our aircraft were too expensive and high tech to be reliable. They told us that we should buy lots and lots of "cheap" aircraft...aerial cannon fodder...which would match the enemy more closely in numbers.

The Vietnam War has been referred to as the "10,000 Day War." Operation DESERT STORM will be known as the "1,000 Hour War." In that thousand hours, all the arguments against the effectiveness of airpower and worth of our expensive high technology weapons were repudiated. It has been said that Generals always fight the "last" war. DESERT STORM proved this wrong — it was not Vietnam. From the President on down the Chain of Command, great pains were taken to make sure that this war would be fought under conditions which favored the Allied Coalition and on the Coalition's time table. President George Bush proclaimed that,

(Overleaf) This C-130 of the 435th Tactical Airlift Wing carried nose art which sent a challenge, not only to Iraq, but to all the critics of airpower since the end of the Second World War.

ISBN 0-89747-260-8

If you have any photographs of the aircraft, armor, soldiers or ships of any nation, particularly wartime snapshots, why not share them with us and help make Squadron/Signal's books all the more interesting and complete in the future. Any photograph sent to us will be copied and the original returned. The donor will be fully credited for any photos used. Please send them to:

Squadron/Signal Publications, Inc.
1115 Crowley Drive.
Carrollton, TX 75011-5010.

"The military will not fight with one hand tied behind their backs...it will not be another Vietnam!" — and it was not!

When Saddam Hussein ordered his army to invade neighboring Kuwait on 2 August 1990, the world expressed outrage. President Bush took the lead in organizing a coalition of twenty-eight nations which opposed the Iraqi annexation of Kuwait. He pressed the United Nations to impose sanctions on Iraq and to issue resolutions that called for the immediate Iraqi withdrawal from Kuwait and payment of war reparations. He backed up these demands by ordering the immediate deployment of over 200,000 U.S. troops to Saudi Arabia, under Operation DESERT SHIELD.

The purpose of the operation was to ensure that Iraq did not invade Saudi Arabia. When Saudi security was assured, the president applied more pressure by ordering a continuation of the military buildup which would give the coalition an offensive capability. He kept the pressure on by insisting on deadlines for Iraqi compliance with the U.N. resolutions. This was designed to deny Iraq room to maneuver on the political and/or propaganda fronts. The president circled his political wagons and made sure that domestic support for the war was assured by a winning a key vote in Congress before going to war. Shortly after the 15 January 1991 final deadline for Iraq to accept the United Nations resolutions passed, Operation DESERT SHIELD became Operation DESERT STORM.

After Vietnam the American military had been brutally honest with itself about enemy capabilities and its own shortcomings. The Air Force, Navy, Army and Marines began to train under more realistic conditions. They developed new tactics to take advantage of technological advances and they developed the right weapons for warfare on the modern battle field. When the time came to use these new weapons and tactics, they overwhelmed the fourth largest army and sixth largest air force in the world in only a few weeks.

F-15C Eagles of the 36th TFW, Bitburg Air Base, Germany, prepare to refuel prior to the second wave of attacks against Iraq. F-15s accounted for the majority of the air-to-air kills against Iraqi aircraft which included: five MiG-29s, seven Mirage F-1s, seven MiG-23s, two MiG-25s, four MiG-21s, two Su-25s, six Su-22s and six helicopters. (USAF by SRA Chris Putman)

An F-15C of the 27th Tactical Fighter Squadron, 1st Tactical Fighter Wing from Langley Air Force Base, Virginia, flies over Iraq. Eagles of the 1st TFW were among the first aircraft deployed to Saudi Arabia as part of DESERT SHIELD. They were quickly followed by fighters from some twenty-seven Tactical Fighter Squadrons from bases across the United States. (USAF by TSGT David McLeod)

The Iraqi Air Force was never a factor in the war. Air Supremacy...a term which may never have been used before...was claimed by the Coalition Air Commander after less than two weeks of combat operations. The old "experts" failed to realize what that new term really meant. It meant that the Coalition Air Forces were free to destroy Iraq's army in the field. The "experts" proclaimed that the inevitable ground war would be bloody and slow. They didn't give airpower the credit for being able to provide meaningful assistance to the ground forces. Additionally, they did not give GEN Schwarzkopf credit for his outstanding planning.

Iraqi leader Saddam Hussein underestimated the effectiveness of a professional fighting force which was well-trained in the use of high technology weapons. He failed to understand that this force had been given a political mandate and popular support which allowed it to unleash the overwhelming force afforded by those weapons. That was one of many mistakes Saddam made, both militarily and politically. Coalition commander GEN H. Norman Schwarzkopf stated that Saddam's biggest mistake was his "absolute predictability." All coalition strategy was based on Hussein's pre-war threats and promises. He was unwavering in his attempts to carry out those threats and as a result, his country has paid a heavy price.

This book is not an in-depth study of the war. Rather, it is a visual survey of much (but not all) of the aerial armada which provided the United States and its Coalition Allies with the greatest military victory since the Second World War and the most lopsided victory in the history of aerial warfare. The 200+ photographs in this book were taken by Official U.S. Air Force photographers. They are supplemented with captions that tell the story of how airpower was used in Operation DESERT STORM. It is also a celebration of the banishment of what has come to be known as "The Vietnam Syndrome" — a feeling that America's military was somehow unable to defeat its enemies.

After Operation DESERT STORM, there can be no doubt that the United States possesses the weapons, the leadership, the highly trained people and the will to ensure that the free peoples of the world will remain free. During the last decade, there was a bumper sticker slogan which was very popular with American military aviators. Now we really know what it means when we read the slogan, "Jet Noise — The Sound of Freedom!"

The author wishes to give a special "Thank You" to Major Richard Cole, USAF, for his assistance in preparing this book.

OPERATION DESERT STORM AIR-TO-AIR KILLS
(Confirmed as of 10 April 1991)

DATE	UNIT	ACFT	TYPE DOWNED	WEAPON USED
17 Jan 91	1 TFW	F-15C	F-1 Mirage	AIM 7
17 Jan 91	33 TFW	F-15C	MiG-29	AIM 7
17 Jan 91	33 TFW	F-15C	F-1 Mirage (2)	AIM 7 (Both)
17 Jan 91	33 TFW	F-15C	MiG-29	AIM 7
17 Jan 91	33 TFW	F-15C	MiG-29	AIM 7
17 Jan 91	VFA-81*	F/A-18 (2)	MiG-21 (2)	AIM 9 (Both)
19 Jan 91	33 TFW	F-15C	MiG-25	AIM 7
19 Jan 91	33 TFW	F-15C	MiG-25	AIM 7
19 Jan 91	33 TFW	F-15C	MiG-29	AIM 7
19 Jan 91	33 TFW	F-15C	MiG-29	Ground Impact
19 Jan 91	36 TFW	F-15C	F-1 Mirage	AIM 7
19 Jan 91	36 FTW	F-15C	F-1 Mirage	AIM 7
26 Jan 91	33 TFW	F-15C	MiG-23	AIM 7
26 Jan 91	33 TFW	F-15C	MiG-23	AIM 7
26 Jan 91	33 TFW	F-15C	MiG-23	AIM 7
27 Jan 91	36 TFW	F-15C	MiG-23 (2)	AIM 9 (Both)
27 Jan 91	36 TFW	F-15C	MiG-23	AIM 7
27 Jan 91	36 TFW	F-15C	F-1 Mirage	AIM 7
29 Jan 91	32 TFS	F-15C	MiG-23	AIM 7
29 Jan 91	33 TFW	F-15C	MiG-23	AIM 7
6 Feb 91	36 TFW	F-15C	Su-25 (2)	AIM 9 (Both)
6 Feb 91	36 TFW	F-15C	MiG-21 (2)	AIM 9 (Both)
6 Feb 91	926 TFG	A-10	Helo (Obs.)	Gun
6 Feb 91	VF-1**	F-14A	Helo (unk type)	AIM 9
7 Feb 91	33 TFW	F-15C	Su-7/17 (2)***	AIM 7 (Both)
7 Feb 91	33 TFW	F-15C	Su-7/17 (2)***	AIM 7 (Both)
7 Feb 91	36 TFW	F-15C	Helo (unk type)	AIM 7
11 Feb 91	36 TFW	F-15C	Helo (unk type)	AIM 7
11 Feb 91	36 TFW	F-15C	Helo (unk type)	AIM 7
15 Feb 91	926 TFG	A-10	MI-8 HIP Helo	Gun
20 Mar 91	36 TFW	F-15C	Su-22	AIM 9
22 Mar 91	36 TFW	F-15C	Su-22	AIM 9

*USS Saratoga
**USS Ranger
***Su-7 and Su-17 are externally similar.

3

An F-15C Eagle of the Royal Saudi Air Force refuels over the Gulf during a DESERT STORM combat air patrol mission. The Eagle carries an air superiority weapons load of four AIM-7 Sparrows on fuselage stations and four AIM-9 Sidewinders on the wing pylons. To extend its time on station, the aircraft carries 610 gallon external fuel tanks on the fuselage centerline and under wing pylons.

A McDonnell-Douglas KC-10A Extender refuels a McDonnell-Douglas F-15C Eagle. The KC-10 was developed from the civil DC-10 transport and is the newest USAF tanker. It is capable of delivering 200,000 pounds of fuel to aircraft during a single mission. The Extender entered service during 1981 and is operated by the Strategic Air Command.

An F-15C Eagle of the 1st Tactical Fighter Wing flies a combat air patrol over Iraq. The Iraqi Air Force was never a factor in the air war. Whenever they came up, they were shot down. A number of Iraqi aircraft were lost attempting to challenge coalition air forces while others were lost fleeing to Iran. 137 Iraqi aircraft, including fighters, attack aircraft, transports and some Iraqi Airways aircraft, did manage to find safe haven in Iran, where they were interned — perhaps permanently.

F-15Cs of the 33rd Tactical Fighter Wing escort a Northrop F-5E Tiger II of the Royal Saudi Air Force during a practice mission leading up to DESERT STORM. During the early stages of DESERT SHIELD, pilots had difficulty getting used to the peculiar characteristics of desert flying. One problem was that the horizon often became indistinct because of blowing sand and dust. (USAF by SRA Chris Putman)

An F-15C takes off to begin a night combat air patrol. The initial air attack that opened Operation DESERT STORM was carried out at night and the Coalition's superiority was never more evident than at night. In addition to radar/communications jamming and Stealth fighters, the allies were aided by Iraqi incompetence. During one early raid, American pilots watched in disbelief as one Iraqi MiG-29 shot down another Iraqi MiG-29, then crashed into the desert. (USAF by SRA Rodney Kern)

An F-15E Strike Eagle of the 4th Tactical Fighter Wing, based at Seymour Johnson Air Force Base, South Carolina. Two squadrons from the 4th TFW deployed to Saudi Arabia and participated in Operation DESERT STORM, the 335th and 336th Tactical Fighter Squadrons. Both units were heavily engaged in the early missions over Iraq aimed at knocking out fixed Scud surface-to-surface missile launch sites. Scud missile sites, storage bunkers and support facilities were high priority targets throughout the air war.

Ground crewmen load AIM-7 Sparrow air-to-air missiles on the fuselage stations of an F-15C Eagle. The AIM-7 is an 'all aspect' radar guided missile, which means that it can be fired from any angle. The missiles on the wing pylon are AIM-9 Sidewinder infrared guided missiles.

An F-15C Eagle of the 1st Tactical Fighter Wing peels off, heading for a target in Iraq. The aircraft is armed with four AIM-7F Sparrows and four AIM-9 Sidewinder air-to-air missiles and carries three drop tanks.

A Strike Eagle pilot climbs on board his F-15E for a DESERT STORM sortie. The aircraft is equipped with conformal fuel tanks, known as Fast Packs. The aircraft is overall Gun Gray. The Air Force lost two F-15Es during DESERT STORM, both during the first days of the war.

An F-15E Strike Eagle refuels from a Boeing KC-135 Stratotanker. The USAF operates a fleet of over 600 tanker aircraft. Fully half of the tanker force was involved in DESERT STORM in support of the strike aircraft.

This F-15E Strike Eagle of the 4th Tactical Fighter Wing is equipped with a LANTIRN night navigation/targeting system pod under the intake. Using this system, the Strike Eagles became an effective quick reaction force to knock out mobile Scud launchers. F-15Es flew "Scud patrols" which were designed to immediately attack the missile sites when they fired.

The F-15E was designed as a long range attack aircraft for interdiction missions under all weather conditions and first flew during August 1981. The Strike Eagle has advanced avionics including moving map displays, synthetic aperture radar, terrain following radar, Forward Looking Infrared (FLIR), Low Altitude Navigation and Targeting Infrared for Night (LANTIRN), and weapons displays on one of three CRTs in the rear cockpit.

With afterburners lit, an F-15E Strike Eagle departs its "deployed location" (Air Force jargon for a classified location) in Saudi Arabia. F-15Es flew forty to sixty sorties per night searching for mobile Scud launchers. They carried a wide variety of weapons including Cluster Bomb Units like the CBU-52, CBU-58, CBU-87, and Mk-20 Rockeyes.

4th Tactical Fighter Wing ground crewmen wash away the residue of a Saudi sandstorm from the surfaces of an F-15E. Mission readiness rates during DESERT STORM exceeded normal peacetime rates due, in large part, to the "surge" efforts of maintenance and weapons personnel.

Ground crewmen remove the chocks from an F-15E of the 4th Tactical Fighter Wing. One of the principal exterior differences between the Strike Eagle and other F-15s are the conformal fuel tanks fitted with tangental weapons pylons. The extra fuel allows for long range interdiction missions. The Strike Eagle can carry some 24,500 pounds of bombs.

An F-15C of the RSAF takes off on a DESERT STORM combat air patrol sortie. Saudi Arabia acquired forty-six F-15Cs and sixteen F-15Ds under Project *Peace Sun* with the first aircraft being delivered on 11 August 1981. CAPT Ayedh al-Shamrani is credited with the downing of two Iraqi Mirage F-1s (with Sidewinders) as the Exocet armed Iraqis headed for Allied ships in the Persian Gulf.

SAC had resurrected the tradition of applying nose art to aircraft in their tanker force long before Operation DESERT SHIELD/DESERT STORM. These KC-135s *SWEET SIXTEEN*, *QUANAH PARKER*, *OL LIGHTNEN* and others participated in the Gulf Air War. Besides regular SAC tanker wings, the Air National Guard and Air Force Reserve provided tankers from the 128th ARG, 134th ARG, 151st ARG, 157th ARG, 160th ARG, 161st ARG, 170th ARG, 190th ARG, 101st ARW 126th ARW, 141st ARW, and 171st ARW of the ANG and the 434th ARW, 452nd ARW, 916th ARG and 940th ARG of the AFRES.

Desert Phoenix was a Lockheed C-130 Hercules transport assigned as an in-theater transport in support of Operation DESERT SHIELD/DESERT STORM. The transports were drawn from regular and reserve units across the U.S.

Some of Tactical Air Command's C-130s also carried nose art. They included the M-16 toting *Sand Surfer*; an aggressive Iraq-eating Bulldog; the laid back *Sand SHARK* with his "Lifes a Beach" hat and 1878 beer can; *DONATELLO*, a Desert Ninja assigned to the 435th TAW; and Roger Rabbit. Regular Air Force C-130s were drawn from the 435th TAW at Rhein Main, Germany, the 317th TAW, Pope AFB and the 314th TAW, Little Rock AFB. The Air National Guard and Air Force Reserve C-130s came from several units. The C-130 was the primary in-theater transport for the Air Force and the only C-130 combat loss of DESERT STORM was an AC-130 gunship which was shot down with the loss of all fourteen crew members.

Nose art was carried by aircraft other than transports such as *Smooth Character*, an RF-4C Phantom II of 117th Tactical Reconnaissance Wing based at Birmingham, Alabama. The nose art was painted on the aircraft by the aircraft's Crew Chief, SSGT James Daily. The aircraft also carries an Air Force Outstanding Unit Award ribbon on the nose. (USAF by TSGT Marvin Lynchard)

The Lockheed C-141 Starlifter played a major role in the USAF airlift for Operation DESERT SHIELD/DESERT STORM. The Military Airlift Command (MAC) moved 72,000 tons of equipment and 91,000 personnel to Saudi Arabia within the first thirty days of DESERT SHIELD. It was done by pressing all available aircraft into service, including those that just completed overhaul and were about to be repainted.

The official Air Force caption read: "FOD damage to a C-141B Starlifter." No other details were given, but whatever foreign object took out this section from the C-141 must have been very impressive! (USAF by CMSgt Don Sutherland)

A lineman directs an RC-135 reconnaissance aircraft into its parking spot. The RC-135s operated alongside other RC-135s equipped with Joint-STARS, an array of sensors which can detect, locate, classify and track moving targets up to 150 miles away. Two prototype Joint-STARS aircraft were deployed to Saudi Arabia and flown by the 4411th Joint-STARS squadron.

A Boeing E-3A Airborne Warning And Control System (AWACS) of the 552nd Airborne Warning and Control Wing, Tinker AFB, Oklahoma provided air traffic control for strike aircraft over Iraq. AWACS is able to identify low level targets at 200 miles and longer ranges for high altitude targets. AWACS provided vectors for F-15s against Iraqi aircraft for intercepts. The RSAF also operates AWACS aircraft.

The world-champion airlifter is the gigantic Lockheed C-5A Galaxy, which has a gross takeoff weight in excess of 764,000 pounds. 435th TAW fuels personnel refuel a C-5 on the ramp at Rhein Main Air Base, Germany prior to a resupply flight to the Persian Gulf. The USAF lost one C-5 on a mission from Germany to the Gulf. (USAF by SRA Michael Eyer)

The E-3 Sentry (AWACS) was built from 1976 to 1984. Thirty-five were built for the USAF, eighteen for NATO, five for Saudi Arabia, seven for the United Kingdom and four for France. The thirty foot rotodome is mounted eleven feet above the fuselage and contains an AN/APY-1 surveillance radar and an IFF/TADIL C antenna.

Lockheed EC-130H Compass Call electronic warfare aircraft of the 41st Electronic Control Squadron are usually based at Davis Monthan Air Force Base, Arizona. The EC-130s were part of the electronic force that blinded the Iraqi Air Force and silenced its communications network.

CAPT Mavis Compagno (aircraft commander) and LT Eric Ross (co-pilot) fly a KC-135R tanker of the 340th Aerial Refueling Wing. DESERT STORM was the first war in which women actively participated as pilots. Despite the congressional mandate to the contrary, some women experienced combat and even became POWs. (USAF by TSGT Perry Heimer)

An Air National Guard C-130E Hercules flies over the Saudi desert. The aircraft is in the European Lizard camouflage that is definitely out of place over the desert.

An E-3 flies over rugged mideastern terrain during a DESERT STORM mission. AWACS provided vital control and coordination throughout the entire war, where coalition air forces flew more than 110,000 sorties. Both E-3B and E-3C aircraft flew missions with the 552nd Wing, accumulating over 5,000 hours in over 375 missions during DESERT SHIELD/DESERT STORM operations. They coordinated missions with their Saudi AWACS counterparts.

SAC KC-135s line up on the taxiway prepared to take off on a refueling mission with Navy and/or Marine aircraft as is evidenced by the drogue and basket attached to the refueling boom. While USAF aircraft are equipped with female refueling receptacles, Navy and Marine aircraft employ the probe and drogue method of refueling. The pace of DESERT STORM missions required supplementing Navy and Marine refueling assets with USAF tankers.

Maintenance personnel of the 335th Tactical Fighter Squadron, 4th Tactical Fighter Wing were transported from Seymour Johnson Air Force Base to Saudi Arabia by a KC-10. (USAF by SSGT Robert Jackson)

An EC-130H of the 41st Electronic Control Squadron is refueled by a KC-135 of the 350th ARS. Electronic aircraft probed Iraqi defenses so often in the months leading up to DESERT STORM that the Iraqis turned off their air defense radars during November in order to deny electronic intelligence more information. (USAF by TSGT H. Deffner)

Maintenance troops prepare to change a tire on *Dust Devil*, a Lockheed C-130E Hercules of the 435th Tactical Airlift Wing.

This KC-135 of the 9th SRW based at Beale AFB was decorated with Santa's sleigh pulled by camels for a Christmas supply mission to the Persian Gulf. (USAF by TSGT H.H. Deffner)

A SAC KC-10 departs for a DESERT STORM refueling mission. Much of the strategic bombing of Iraq occurred at night and was preceded by refueling of the strike aircraft so that they entered enemy airspace with full tanks.

A Marine Corps AH-1W SuperCobra lands on the deck of the amphibious assault ship USS NASSAU (LHA-4). One of the great deceptions of the war was the well-publicized Marine amphibious landing force poised in the northern Persian Gulf for a landing on Kuwaiti beaches. This force, although never used, forced the Iraqis to maintain troops in positions to defend the beaches. (USN by PH1 Olson)

(Left) Ground crews perform maintenance on a Marine Bell AH-1W SuperCobra at their base in Saudi Arabia which was known as LZ-32 Site Alpha. The SuperCobras were armed with TOW or Hellfire anti-tank missiles in addition to their 20MM M197 turreted cannon. The fairing over the stub wing is a chaff/flare launcher.

A pair of Marine AH-1W SuperCobras escort a UH-1N Huey on a reconnaissance mission over their Area of Operations. The SuperCobra is the latest AH-1 Cobra variant which was originally introduced during the Vietnam War (AH-1G). The AH-1W is powered by two 1,723 shp T700-GE-401 engines.

Bell AH-1W SuperCobras parked on the ramp at their deployed location in Saudi Arabia. The AH-1Ws were used to provide close air support for the Marines when the ground war got underway, using TOW missiles to destroy enemy strong points.

(Left) A CH-46 Sea Knight of HC-5 DET 5 (operating off the USNS SPICA) delivers a sling load of cargo to the flight deck of the hospital ship USNS MERCY during Operation DESERT SHIELD. (USN by PH1 R.J. Oriez)

A Marine CH-46 Sea Knight of HMM-165 lands aboard the battleship USS WISCONSIN on 6 February 1991. Members of the Coalition forces flew aboard to attend briefings with CAPT D.S. Bill III, commanding officer of the WISCONSIN, which provided fire support against targets in Kuwait and southern Iraq. (USN by PH2 Robert Clare)

The MH-53J Pave Low Enhanced Super Jolly Green Giant rescue helicopter provided long range rescue capability for crews downed behind enemy lines. The MH-53J is equipped with an inertial navigation system, stabilized FLIR, Doppler navigation equipment, radar from an A-7D Corsair II and a computer projected moving map display. The first of the improved Jolly Greens was delivered to the USAF during 1987.

(Left) Marine ground crewmen rush to rearm a Bell AH-1W SuperCobra with TOW anti-tank missiles during DESERT STORM combat operations. Most Marine SuperCobras carried four to eight TOWs and 2.75 inch rocket pods.

A Hellfire missile armed Marine AH-1W SuperCobra takes off for a ground support mission during DESERT STORM. For countermeasures, the AH-1Ws were equipped with chaff/flare launchers on the stub wings and a DISCO light IR jammer behind the main rotor.

Marine Corps CH-46 Sea Knights were used to fly men and equipment from the LHA/LPH assault ships to airfields in Saudi Arabia. Later they were repainted in a Sand and Brown camouflage. The aircraft were armed with .50 caliber machine guns in the cabin windows, one on each side.

A desert camouflaged USAF MH-60G Pave Hawk rescue helicopter on the ramp at its Saudi base. The Pave Hawks were modified from UH-60As and are equipped with Doppler/INS, electronic moving map display, Tacan, RDR-14 lightweight weather/ground mapping radar, secure HF and Satcom, .50 caliber machine guns, a Pave Low III Forward Looking Infrared and an aerial refueling boom.

A French ALAT Gazelle helicopter flies over the desert. This helicopter was operated by one of the seven French Army helicopter units stationed at Hafar Al Batine in Saudi Arabia.

Marine Corps CH-46Es were operated by HMM-161, HMM-263 and HMM-265. The Sea Knights were used to shuttle men and supplies from the various LPH and LHA amphibious assault ships in the Gulf and their shore base at Dhahran.

The Boeing Vertol CH-46 carries a crew of three and is capable of lifting 4,000 pounds of cargo. Different variants of the Sea Knight have been in service with the Navy and Marines since the early 1960s.

A Navy CH-46E Sea Knight of HC-5 shuttles supplies from USS SYLVANIA to USS JOHN F. KENNEDY on 21 January 1991. Sea Knights are the primary vert-rep (vertical replenishment) helicopter in service with the composite helicopter squadrons. (USCG by PA1 Chuck Kalnbach)

This desert camouflaged UH-60A Blackhawk is assigned to the Royal Saudi Land Forces. The RSLF operates a total of eighteen Blackhawks which were based at Dhahran.

This U.S. Army UH-60 Blackhawk is equipped with ESSS bolt-on stub wings. These wings are capable of mounting external fuel tanks and/or Hellfire anti-tank guided missiles. The Blackhawk also mounts two M60 machine guns, one on each side.

UH-60 Blackhawks of the 2nd Battalion, 82nd Aviation Brigade airlift two 105mm Howitzers of C Battery, 1st of the 319th Air Field Artillery Regiment. (US Army by Brian Cumper)

A UH-60 Blackhawk of the Royal Saudi Land Forces. The Blackhawk is one of the aircraft fighting in its first war. The U.S. Army procurement of the Blackhawk was planned at 2,251 aircraft. Currently, variants of the Blackhawk are also operated by the USAF, Navy, and Marines, along with several foreign air forces.

Apaches fired the first shots of the war, attacking Iraqi early warning radar sites at 0238 on 17 January 1991. *Task Force Normandy* was made up of eight Apaches and a UH-60. The AH-64s opened a hole in the Iraqi air defense radar net which allowed 100 strike aircraft to make undetected attacks on targets in Baghdad. Using Hellfire missiles, the AH-64s attacked power supplies, communications equipment and radar dishes (in that order). Apaches were also used for reconnaissance missions, since their night vision devices enabled them to acquire targets beyond 12 kilometers and verify identification at 7 kilometers.

The McDonnell Douglas AH-64 Apache attack helicopter was one of the most maligned modern weapons systems. It was the target of numerous journalists, who claimed that it would not stand up to the rigors of modern combat. DESERT STORM operations proved that the Apache worked and worked well. It had the highest combat readiness rate of any Army rotary wing aircraft in the theater and was operated by the 82nd Airborne Division, the 101st Airborne Division, the 2nd Armored Division and the 1st Cavalry Division.

SH-3H Sea King anti-submarine helicopters were operated by HS-11, aboard USS AMERICA (CV-66) and HS-9, aboard USS THEODORE ROOSEVELT (CVN-71). The Sea Kings operate in both the anti-submarine and rescue roles.

These UH-60 Blackhawk helicopters are being prepared for shipment from Fort Bragg, North Carolina to Saudi Arabia during the early stages of Operation DESERT SHIELD.

A-10A Thunderbolt II (Warthog) attack aircraft of the 23rd TFW, England AFB, Louisiana, the 354th TFW, Myrtle Beach AFB, South Carolina and the 10th TFW, RAF Lakenheath, England deployed to Saudi Arabia for DESERT STORM. The A-10 has been affectionately dubbed the Warthog by its pilots. This A-10 is armed with a pair of Maverick missiles and a pair of AIM-9 Sidewinder as it moves into position to take on fuel on 3 February 1991. (USAF by TSGT Rose Reynolds)

A-10s of the 355th TFS flew most of their missions at night. By the third week of the war, so many Iraqi tanks and armored vehicles had been destroyed that it was difficult to acquire "good" targets. On one mission, A-10s of the 355th caught a column of Iraqi armor at al Wafra and destroyed twenty-four tanks. Anti-tank weapons included the infrared-homing Maverick, Rockeye CBUs and the 30MM GAU-8 cannon. (USAF by TSGT Marvin Lynchard)

A sharkmouthed A-10A of the 23rd Tactical Fighter Wing is hot-refueled between missions. The 23rd was based at the Royal Saudi Air Force base at Tabouk during DESERT SHIELD. A-10s worked with Forward Air Controllers (FACs) flying USAF OA-10s and Marine OV-10s. They were supported by defense suppression F-4G Wild Weasels in their attacks against Iraqi armor.

A-10s of the 23rd TFW taxi in after a DESERT STORM mission. The USAF lost five A-10s in combat. Air Force Reserve A-10 pilot CAPT Robert Swain of the 706th TFS scored the first A-10 air-to-air kill when he shot down an Iraqi helicopter. He fired a long burst of 30mm fire from a mile away and destroyed the aircraft. The GAU-8 is a seven barrel cannon and fires a depleted uranium round which will penetrate any armor.

An A-10 of the 23rd is refueled between missions. It is armed with Cluster Bomb Units, Mavericks and AIM-9 Sidewinders. The Warthog can carry up to 16,000 pounds of ordnance on eleven external stations. In addition to IR Mavericks, the A-10 can also carry the laser guided Maverick guided by the Pave Penny pod mounted on the starboard side of the nose.

The AGM-65D IR-Maverick, when equipped with Hughes IIR seeker, can lock on to targets at long ranges. The weapon was especially effective in the low-humidity of the Saudi/Kuwaiti desert. It weighs 635 pounds at launch and accelerates to supersonic speed (at ranges beyond a half mile).

This Warthog is armed with a varied ordnance load including 500 pound bombs, Maverick anti-tank missiles and Sidewinder AAMs. It also carries an AN/ALQ-119 jamming pod on the starboard outboard pylon. The 353rd and 355th Tactical Fighter Squadrons of the 354th Fighter Wing operated from Al Jubayl during DESERT SHIELD/DESERT STORM.

23

This A-10 Thunderbolt II of the 23rd TFW carried two interesting sentiments on the inside of the boarding ladder access door. *Live Free or Die* was probably applied before the war, but *IRAQ CROSS THE LINE AND YOUR ASS IS MINE* is much more timely...and prophetic.

The tradition of decorating combat aircraft with imaginative artwork was carried on during DESERT STORM. This A-10 is being painted with a fortune teller who sees dire consequences for the enemy in her crystal ball.

PANTHER was an A-10 of the 353rd Tactical Fighter Squadron. Besides its nickname, the crew has penned more profound sentiments on the boarding ladder door.

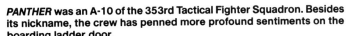

This A-10 Thunderbolt II carried the well known cartoon character of Bart Simpson surfing on a Rockeye cluster bomb unit which is identified as a "Mk-20 Mod-7 247 Mk 118 Mod-0 anti-tank bombs".

The sexy blonde on this A-10 was known as *Little Lady Diane*. She also carried the name *PLAY TIME*.

Air Force artists painted a variety of nose art on A-10s, ranging from traditional pinup art to the grim reality of the air-to-ground war waged by the Thunderbolt II.

The F-4 Phantom distinguished itself in yet another war. These RF-4Cs of the 171st TRG carried sharkmouth markings and two tone Gray camouflage. The reconnaissance Phantoms played an important role in DESERT STORM because satellites could not provide timely intelligence data, the SR-71 had been retired and the Advanced Tactical Airborne Reconnaissance System (ATARS) was still in the lab because of defense cuts.

Another version of the Phantom which saw service in the Gulf was the F-4G Wild Weasel defense suppression aircraft. The F-4G's main weapon was the AGM-88A Highspeed Anti-Radiation Missile (HARM). It has a launch weight of 807 pounds and achieves a speed of over Mach 2. In the self defense mode, the missile detects any emissions from radar sites, locks on to the site within milliseconds and can be launched against the site.

SSGT James Daily, an RF-4C crew chief of the 117 CAM Squadron, Alabama Air National Guard, performs post flight inspection on his Phantom. The RF-4s used KA-56 panoramic, horizon to horizon cameras and an IR line scanner to provide intelligence information. (USAF by TSGT Marvin Lynchard)

An F-4G of the 52nd TFW, from Spangdahlem AB, Germany on 1 March 1991. The aircraft is armed with AGM-88A HARMs. During DESERT SHIELD the Wild Weasel F-4s were part of the strike package that would approach Iraqi defenses at high speed, then turn away. This allowed F-4Gs to map and analyze the defenses in preparation for the war.

These sharkmouthed RF-4Cs of the Alabama Air National Guard taxi in after a DESERT STORM reconnaissance mission. They both carry an ALQ-131 jamming pod on the port inboard wing pylon.

This F-4G Wild Weasel crew signals their success in attacking Iraqi Surface-To-Air Missile (SAM) sites around Baghdad early in the air war. The F-4G configuration was a modification of the F-4E airframe which replaced the nose mounted 20MM Vulcan rotary cannon with electronics equipment.

This F-4G of the 561st Tactical Fighter Squadron, 35th Tactical Fighter Wing is normally based at George AFB, California. The Phantom is on an anti-radar mission armed with two HARM missiles on the inboard pylons during DESERT STORM. The 561st operated from Muharraq Air Base during the war. (USAF by TSGT Hans Deffner)

27

An RF-4C of the 117th TRG, Alabama ANG taxies in after a mission. Bulges on either side of the nose camera window are for Radar Homing and Warning (RHAW) antenna. The aircraft carries a jammer pod under the inboard wing pylon.

An RF-4C of the 152nd Tactical Reconnaissance Group approaches a tanker during a DESERT STORM mission. Other RF-4Cs from the 67th Tactical Reconnaissance Wing, based at Bergstrom AFB, Texas also participated in DESERT STORM.

The F-4G is the only Phantom still flown by units of the active Air Force. This Wild Weasel Phantom, approaching a tanker on 2 March 1991, is armed with AGM-88A HARM missiles. The large fairing under the nose contains the APR-38 subsystems for radar homing and warning (RHAW) gear. (USAF by TSGT Rose Reynolds)

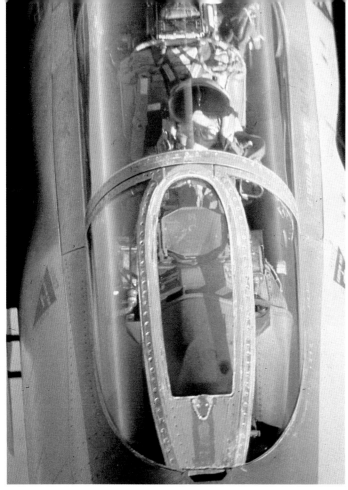

A Phantom pilot eyeballs the "boomer" (refueling boom operator) of a KC-135 tanker during a refueling mission. In spite of its age, the Phantom was still a Mach 2 aircraft. Ironically, it was during Operation DESERT STORM that the USAF announced plans to retire the F-4, replacing it with the F-16s in the Wild Weasel role.

An F-111F of the 48th Tactical Fighter Wing, RAF Lakenheath, England refuels enroute to attack an Iraqi target. It is armed with a pair of GBU-15 electro-optical "smart" bombs which will be guided to the target by the AN/AVG-26 Pave Tack laser designator carried on the forward center-line fuselage station.

F-111Fs are escorted by an EF-111 Raven on a low level practice mission during Operation DESERT SHIELD on 12 November 1990. F-111s were based at Taif, Incirlik, Turkey, and RAF Akrotiri during DESERT SHIELD/DESERT STORM. (USAF by TSGT Rose Reynolds)

A pair of EF-111A Ravens of the 390th Electronic Combat Squadron, 366th Tactical Fighter Wing fly over a rugged mountainous area. The aircraft are home based at Mountain Home AFB, Idaho. EF-111s of the 42nd Electronic Combat Squadron, based at RAF Upper Heyford, United Kingdom, also participated in the war.

48th TFW F-111s are refueled by a KC-10 Extender. The official USAF caption states that they are returning from their first combat missions over Iraq and Kuwait. They are armed with AIM-9 Sidewinders on the inboard pylons and carry ALQ-131 jamming pods under the forward fuselage. (USAF by SRA Chris Putman)

An F-111F of the 493rd TFS, 48th TFW taxies in at its base in Saudi Arabia. The F-111F was the last version produced. Some of the most dramatic bomb damage video was produced by the Pave Tack pod turret carried on the underside of the F-111F. The seeker swivels and pivots to remain locked on the target as the F-111 maneuvers away from the target.

An F-111F crew is saluted by their Crew Chief as they taxi out of their hardened aircraft shelter for another combat mission. The F-111 is loaded with GBU-15 and Paveway Laser Guided Bombs (LGBs).

F-111s line up for refueling during DESERT SHIELD. They carry the smart bombs they will later employ during DESERT STORM. The F-111 was first introduced in the 1960s and it is still a potent and sophisticated weapons system. It is capable of speeds up to Mach 2.2 and has a service ceiling (clean) of 60,000 feet.

An EF-111F Raven taxies out for a mission over Iraq. EF-111s escorted strike groups of F-111F bombers providing jamming support against air defense radars.

An F-111F Aardvark taxies back to its revetment at Taif Air Base during Operation DESERT SHIELD, while an EF-111 moves along another taxiway. The two types operated together from the base.

This F-111F of the 48th Tactical Fighter Wing was loaded with 500 pound Mk 82 bombs, an ALQ-131 jamming pod, and the Pave Tack system for a practice mission during Operation DESERT SHIELD.

An F-111F of the 494th TFS, 48th TFW after a mission over Iraq. It is carrying a Cluster Bomb Unit on the inboard pylon. F-111s did much of their bombing against strategic targets deep inside Iraq, using their all-weather capabilities.

EF-111 Ravens of the 366th TFW refuel during a practice mission as part of Operation DESERT SHIELD on 12 November 1990. The EF-111 was a conversion of the F-111F and all development work was done by Grumman. EF-111s of the 390th Electronic Combat Squadron were the first coalition aircraft to penetrate Iraqi airspace at the beginning of DESERT STORM. The EF-111s were challenged by MIG-29s and MIG-25s as they preceded the attack forces of DESERT STORM into Iraqi airspace by a half an hour, but none were lost to enemy action. (USAF by TSGT Rose Reynolds)

An EF-111 Raven is parked outside of its shelter in Saudi Arabia. EF-111s were used for close-in jamming of Iraqi defenses as part of the strike package. The jamming was effective, since AAA was fired at noise and SAMs were launched in an unguided mode.

33

One of the most prolific DESERT STORM attack aircraft was the General Dynamics F-16 Fighting Falcon. Air Force F-16 units that participated in the war were: the 50th TFW, Hahn AB, Germany; 363rd TFW, Shaw AFB, South Carolina; 388th TFW, Hill AFB, Utah; 401st TFW, Torrejon AB, Spain; 347th TFW, Moody AFB, Georgia and the 174th TFW, Hancock Field, N.Y. The F-16s were based at Al Dhafra, Al Mindhat, Diyarbakir and Doha. When F-16s deployed to Saudi Arabia, one of the first units to go deployed all twenty-four aircraft with no aborts and all twenty-four arrived together after a sixteen hour flight with ten refuelings. It was the longest F-16 flight on record. F-16s were often used in large strike packages of up to sixty aircraft including F-15 fighter cover, EF-111 Jammers, and F-4G Wild Weasels. Five F-16s were lost in combat and two were lost in non-combat missions during the war.

A crew chief of the 363rd Tactical Fighter Wing from Shaw Air Force Base, South Carolina, pulls maintenance on an F-16 in one of the unit's hardened aircraft shelters at Al Dhafra. Though capable of defending itself in air-to-air combat, the F-16 was used almost exclusively in the air-to-ground role, with F-15C Eagles providing air cover against Iraqi interceptors. F-15s shot down two MiG-29 Fulcrums which threatened an F-16 strike package on the first day of the war.

Two flights of F-16 bombers taxi out for takeoff prior to a DESERT STORM mission. Many Fighting Falcon missions were flown by Air Force Reserve or Air National Guard units.

F-16s of the 363rd Tactical Fighter Wing line up behind a KC-135 tanker to take on fuel after a strike mission.

F-16As of the 138th Tactical Fighter Squadron, 174th Tactical Fighter Group, "The Boys From Syracuse," New York Air National Guard line up for a mission. The Falcons are armed with 2,000 pound bombs.

An F-16C of the 17th TFS, 363rd TFW lines up to take on fuel enroute to Iraq. It is armed with a CBU-87 and carries an AN/ALQ-119 jamming pod. This pod suffered a high rate of failure initially (one crew chief painted Black pods on his F-16 every time a pod failed) but as experience with the pods built up their reliability increased.

An F-16 of the 388th TFW enroute to Saudi Arabia as part of Operation DESERT SHIELD from Hill AFB, Utah. They are configured for long range and/or air defense with four Sidewinders and AN/ALQ-131 jamming pods. (USAF by TSGT Marvin D. Lynchard)

F-16s of the 50th TFW, Hahn AB, Germany are loaded with 2,000 pound bombs for a mission against Iraq. They carry ALQ-131 pods on the centerline. Despite heavy bombing and jamming of Iraqi early warning radars, AAA and SAMs continued to be a severe threat during the air war. The pods, combined with effective tactics, kept coalition air losses to a minimum.

An F-16C of the 614th TFS, 401st TFW taxies out for a DESERT STORM mission past a Mirage F-1 of the Free Kuwiat Air Force. Coalition pilots quickly learned that dropping their weapons from altitudes of 10,000 to 15,000 feet enabled them to remain out of range of much of the anti-aircraft fire.

A Fighting Falcon of the 421st TFS 'Black Widows,' 388th TFW loaded with CBUs for a DESERT STORM mission. As the third phase of the air war got underway in earnest, aircraft began attacking dug-in Iraqi troops with CBUs. The Iraqis responded by deploying decoys to blunt the force of the coalition air attacks.

An F-16A of the 157th TFS, South Carolina Air National Guard. The 157th operated twenty-five F-16s with forty pilots. They formed part of the 4th Tactical Fighter Wing (Provisional), a unit comprised of several National Guard fighter squadrons.

An F-16 of the 401st TFW taxies past French Air Force Mirage F-1s. The French operated the Mirage F-1 in the air defense and fighter escort roles.

An F-16 moves into position to take on fuel from a KC-135 of the 171st ARW of the Pennsylvania Air Guard. It is armed with CBU-59/B Rockeye cluster bombs loaded with 7 PLU-77/B anti-personnel and anti-material bomblets.

An F-16C of the 4th TFS, 388th TFW. The C model incorporated several advances in avionics over the A model, including a Westinghouse APG-68 multi-mode radar, new cockpit displays, a GEC Avionics wide angle head-up-display (HUD) with forward-looking infrared (FLIR) video and increased memory for its mission computers.

F-16s of the 363rd TFW parked on the ramp outside of their hardened, "drive through" shelters at their Saudi air base.

An F-16C of the 347th TFW based at Moody AFB, Georgia. It is equipped with an ALQ-131 jamming pod on the centerline and the LANTIRN pod on the port side of the intake. LANTIRN equipped F-16s of the 347th TFW and the 388th TFW participated in DESERT STORM. F-16 pilots call the LANTIRN F-16 "the poor man's F-15E" because of its smaller size and payload. The F-16's computer automatically holds the aircraft at 200 feet, while the pilot searched for targets. The LANTIRN pods were extremely reliable and effective in the low humidity of the desert.

An F-16C of the 363rd Tactical Fighter Wing lands after a large scale raid on the fourth day of DESERT STORM. (USAF by TSGT Perry Heimer)

An F-16C Fighting Falcon of the 17th Tactical Fighter Squadron, 363rd Tactical Fighter Wing enroute to bomb the Iraqi Republican Guards in Kuwait. It is armed with Cluster Bomb Units, AIM-9 Sidewinder air-to-air missiles for self defense, and carried external fuel tanks. The pilot has started a mission scorecard under the canopy. (USAF by TSGT Perry Heimer)

(Left) LTC Billy Diehl of the 363rd Tactical Fighter Wing moves his F-16C into position to take on fuel while enroute to targets in Kuwait. The F-16s were heavily involved in ground attack missions against dug in Iraqi troops and armor. (USAF by TSGT Perry Heimer)

A 388th TFW Falcon slides away from the tanker after taking on fuel while enroute to targets in Kuwait on 2 March 1991. It is armed with Rockeye Cluster Bomb Units for strikes against dug in Iraqi troops near the Saudi-Kuwaiti border. (USAF by TSGT Marvin Lynchard)

Ground crewmen still like to paint messages for the enemy on bombs. This F-16 is armed with 2,000 pound bombs on the wing stations, AIM-9 Sidewinders on the wingtips and an ECM pod on the centerline.

A Lockheed F-117A Stealth Fighter of the 37th TFW, based at the Tonopah Test Range, Nevada, taxies at Langley AFB prior to the unit's departure for Saudi Arabia and Operation DESERT SHIELD. The open auxiliary suck-in doors, just behind the intakes, provide additional air for taxiing and are closed during flight. (USAF MSGT Belcher)

Stealth Fighter technology includes special coatings on the windscreen to deflect radar beams which would otherwise reflect off of the pilot and ejection seat. Other stealth features include radar absorbing paint, the faceting of the fuselage and wing, and shielded intakes and exhaust.

A Stealth fighter is towed from its shelter at Khamis Mushayt for a mission during DESERT STORM. The first F-117A combat squadron was the 415th TFS "Nightstalkers" which became operational in October of 1983. The 416th TFS "Ghost Riders" became operational in January 1984. The F-117's first combat mission was during Operation JUST CAUSE when it attacked Rio Hato, Panama early in the morning of 20 December 1989.

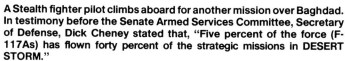

A Stealth fighter pilot climbs aboard for another mission over Baghdad. In testimony before the Senate Armed Services Committee, Secretary of Defense, Dick Cheney stated that, "Five percent of the force (F-117As) has flown forty percent of the strategic missions in DESERT STORM."

Half of the Stealth force lined up at Langley AFB enroute to Saudi Arabia as part of Operation DESERT SHIELD. Later figures released by DOD reveal that 2.5 percent of the air forces struck 31 percent of the targets on the first day of the war.

(Left) Unit pride can be demonstrated by conversion of something as mundane as a parking sign. Stealth fighters used laser-guided 2,000 pound bombs to destroy strategic Iraqi targets, including the air defense headquarters.

F-117s being refueled outside of their shelters in Saudi Arabia. The Stealth Fighters destroyed ninety-five percent of targets struck in and around Baghdad during the war. One of the most memorable hits was on the Iraqi Air Force headquarters building in Baghdad. A laser-guided bomb hit the roof, dead center, and traveled through the multi-story building before detonating in a spectacular fashion. (USAF by TSGT Deffner)

An F-117A is prepared for a mission against targets in Iraq. Some of the significant Iraqi targets destroyed included hardened aircraft shelters, called "impregnable and nuclear proof" by the so-called experts prior to the war. They were usually destroyed by single laser-guided hardened case 2,000 pound bomb. (USAF by TSGT Deffner)

A tow bar is hooked up to an F-117. The Stealth presented no maintenance problems during DESERT SHIELD/DESERT STORM despite its high sortie rate. The F-117 carries its bomb load internally, common weapons being the Paveway II 2,000 pound laser-guided bomb, AGM-130A, GBU-15, SUU-20 and BLU-109.

A Stealth fighter rolls out after a mission with its drag 'chute deployed. Despite its dart-like appearance, the Stealth is a subsonic aircraft with a max speed of .90 Mach (603 mph). GEN Merrill A. McPeak, USAF Chief of Staff, noted that the Iraqi air force had been overwhelmed by a fraction of the coalition force, noting the impunity with which the Stealth fighters operated over Baghdad.

B-52s from the 379th Bomb Wing, Wurtsmith AFB, Michigan take off on 6 February 1991, for a mission against Iraqi targets. B-52s from Castle AFB, California, Loring AFB, Maine, Barksdale AFB, Louisiana, and Griffis AFB, N.Y. also participated in DESERT STORM. The bombing missions were staged from bases in Saudi Arabia, Diego Garcia and RAF Fairford. (USAF by TSGT Rose Reynolds)

A SAC B-52 takes off for a bombing mission. The B-52H has a maximum gross takeoff weight of 488,000 pounds and a range of 8,800 miles. Though many B-52s are as old or older than the crews flying them, their huge bomb load makes them a very effective weapon against dug-in troops.

B-52s lined up on the ramp at their desert base prior to a DESERT STORM mission. They are painted in overall Gunship Gray. One B-52 was lost during DESERT STORM in a non-combat mission on 3 February 1991. Three of the crew of six were rescued from the Persian Gulf.

A B-52H on final approach for landing. The Stratofortress has undergone extensive modification and carries its own electronic counter-measures jamming equipment. Additionally, it carries 192 ALE-20 flares to decoy heat-seeking missiles and 1,125 packages of ALE-24 chaff. The last defensive system is a radar-directed 20MM Vulcan cannon in the tail.

An Ordnance crew loads a 2,000 pound Mk 84 bomb onto an F-16. A lot was made of the difference between "smart" bombs and "dumb" bombs, ignoring the fact that ballistics computers in aircraft such as the F-16 and F/A-18 give the pilot the ability to place free-fall iron bombs on target with great accuracy.

Members of the 1708th MMS load M-117D bombs in the bomb bay of a B-52. The 750 pound M-117D has retarding tail fins indicating that this will be a low-level mission for the BUF. In order to avoid the SAM threat early in the war, many B-52 missions were flown at low altitude. (USAF by SRA Chris Putman)

Armorers load a CBU-87 on an F-16. The cluster bomb unit (CBU) is based on a common dispenser which can be loaded with various sub-munitions. The CBU-87/B dispenser deploys tail fins upon release which cause the bomb to spin. At a pre-set altitude, the case splits apart and 202 CBU-97/B bomblets are discharged.

Ground crews load MK-20 Rockeye CBUs on an F-15E Strike Eagle of the 4th TFW. The MK-20 Rockeye is one of the most widely used CBUs and was first used in the Vietnam War. It weighs 490 pounds and contains 247 M-118 bomblets which are released at an altitude of 500 feet, covering an area of 30,000 square feet.

Armorers reload an A-10A of the 354th TFW between missions. Rockeye CBUs are being loaded and crews are preparing to reload the GAU-8/A Avenger cannon with ammunition. The Avenger system weighs 3,800 pounds when fully loaded, is twenty-one feet long and can be programmed to fire at either 2,100 or 4,200 rounds per minute.

Deck crews load an AGM-88/A Highspeed Anti Radiation Missile (HARM) on the wing pylon of an F/A-18. HARM is used to detect and destroy enemy radars, has a top speed of Mach 2.5 and carries a fragmentation warhead with a proximity fuse. It can be programmed in three different launch modes including self defense, target of opportunity, or pre-briefed.

Ground crews refuel and rearm an F-16 of the 401st Tactical Fighter Wing. The aircraft carries Cluster Bomb Units on the wing pylon and an AIM-9L Sidewinder on the wingtip launcher. The Sidewinder is in Light Gray rather than the usual overall White.

The AIM-9 Sidewinder air-to-air missile (AAM) was the first infrared guided weapon of its kind. It was designed by the Naval Weapons Center at China Lake, California during the late 1940s. The original variants could only be fired from behind an enemy aircraft, since the seeker needed the large heat signature of the engine exhaust to home on. The latest versions of this missile are "all aspect." They are able to sense and lock on to heat sources such as friction-heated leading edges and can be fired from any bearing to the target. The Sidewinder is a "fire and forget" missile. Once its seeker head locks on to a target, it can be launched and will guide without input from the carrier aircraft. This close-range missile is the missile of choice for many fighter pilots because of its reliability.

A ground crewman loads an AIM-7 Sparrow missile on an F-15. The latest version of the Sparrow is the AIM-7M, manufactured by Raytheon and General Dynamics. It has increased resistance to jamming and improved look-down capability. The Sparrow has a range of 62 miles, a launch weight of 503 pounds, and will accelerate out to Mach 4. It is radar-guided and can be launched from beyond visual range.

49

Armorers load Cluster Bomb Units on a Triple Ejector Rack. The TER can hold three CBUs, one on each side and one on the bottom.

The imaging seeker on the infrared Maverick detects targets based on the difference in temperature against the background, making it particularly effective in the desert at night. The infrared image is depicted on a video display in the cockpit after the missile seeker's protective cover is jettisoned from the nose of the Maverick enroute to the target. The seeker head is cooled by a closed-circuit cooler to prevent degradation of the IR image. After the Maverick is locked on to a target and fired, the aircraft can break away. Mavericks are normally fired from low altitude, but climb to assure a final attack trajectory that approaches the target from above, since the weakest tank armor is on top. The 500 pound Maverick is usually supersonic when it hits its target and not even the best enemy armor could survive a Maverick.

Ground crewmen load a CBU on the wing pylon of an F-16. The segmented case of the CBU is evident. Three versions of CBUs were used by F-16s: the CBU-52 for light armor, the CBU-58 for troops and trucks, and the CBU-87 for tanks.

Marine ground crewmen prepare to load a HARM anti-radiation missile on an F/A-18 Hornet strike fighter. Marine ground crews wore their flak jackets and carried their gas masks on the flight line.

Part of the so-called "peace dividend" resulting from the end of the cold war was large stocks of pre-positioned air-to-ground munitions in Europe. These guaranteed that adequate supplies of weapons were available for the forces in Saudi Arabia.

This Mk-84 2,000 pound bomb carries a number of messages from the ground crews. The 2,000 pound bomb makes a good parking lot ground clearer. One of the other sentiments expressed by the loaders was "Today is a good day to die!"

A1C Jennifer Kolb refills her R-9 Kovatch refueling truck at a Saudi base fuel storage facility. A1C Kolb is a refueling operator with the 363rd Supply Squadron, Fuels Management Branch, Shaw AFB, South Carolina. (USAF by SSGT Victor Owens)

51

A-6E Intruders of VA-75 and Rockeye armed A-7Es of VA-46 Clansmen take up position to take on fuel from a KC-135 on 6 February 1991. The A-6E refueled first, then provided tanker service, using the centerline buddy pod, for some of the A-7s. (USAF by TSGT Rose Reynolds)

(Left) An A-6E Intruder of VA-75, Sunday Punchers, of the Red Sea battle group refuels from a KC-135 during a DESERT STORM mission on 29 January 1991. (USAF by SRA Chris Putman)

An F-14A+ Tomcat of VF-103 flying off the USS SARATOGA (CV-60) lines up to take on fuel from an Air Force KC-135 on 4 February 1991. The Tomcat is armed with Phoenix, Sparrow and Sidewinder air-to-air missiles. (USAF by SRA Chris Putman)

An F/A-18 Hornet of VFA-81 Sunliners flying off the USS SARATOGA, moves into position to take on fuel from an Air Force KC-135. The demands of the high sortie rate against Iraq required the help of USAF tanker resources to refuel Navy and Marine Corps fighters. (USAF by SRA Chris Putman)

An F-14 Tomcat of VF-154, from the USS INDEPENDENCE. USS INDEPEN-DENCE was one of the first carriers to arrive in support of Operation DESERT SHIELD, having sailed on 23 June 1990 for a regularly scheduled Mediterranean cruise. Being in the Med, the ship was easily diverted.

A Grumman E-2C Hawkeye of VAW-125 launches from the number four catapult aboard USS SARATOGA. Though a veteran of neary 30 years of service, the E-2 continues to be the Navy version of the AWACS, providing early warning and air control for the fleet.

This F/A-18 of VFA-113 Stingers was flown by the squadron commander CDR Gary Koger "Cricket," off the USS INDEPENDENCE. The McDonnell Douglas F/A-18 Hornet was developed from the Northrop YF-17 lightweight fighter prototype which lost out to the YF-16 in the mid-70s. The Navy lost two Hornets in combat, and one in a non-combat accident during DESERT STORM.

An A-7E of VA-46 Clansmen taxies to the catapult aboard USS JOHN F. KENNEDY. VA-46 and VA-72 flew A-7Es during DESERT STORM. These were probably the last operational missions for the A-7 Corsair II, which is due to be retired.

A Lockheed S-3B Viking of VS-22, off USS JOHN F KENNEDY. The aircraft was pressed into service as a tanker during DESERT STORM carrying a buddy store under the port wing. The S-3's normal mission is anti-submarine warfare.

An F/A-18 of VMFA-333 Shamrocks taxies to its parking spot after a DESERT STORM mission on 4 February 1991. A-6Es of VMA (AW) 224, armed with Rockeye CBUs, are ready to go on a night mission against Iraqi troops in Kuwait. (USAF by MSGT Bill Thompson)

A Marine Corps F/A-18C Hornet of VMFA-232 Red Devils (based at MCAS Kaneohe Bay, Hawaii) taxies out for a DESERT STORM mission armed with HARM anti-radiation missiles on the wing pylons and Sidewinders on the wingtips.

A-6Es of VA-35 and F-14A+s of VF-74 aboard USS SARATOGA during DESERT SHIELD. The A-6 Intruder is the Navy's primary all-weather medium bomber, although overdue for replacement. A-6s are being modified with new composite wings to extend their service lives until a new attack bomber can be placed into service. The Navy lost five A-6s during DESERT STORM, four in combat, and one in an accident.

An F/A-18D of VMFA (AW) 121 Green Knights, the first all weather Marine Corps F/A-18 squadron. The night attack F/A-18D is slated to replace Marine Corps A-6 Intruders. F/A-18s of VMFA-235 and VMFA-314 are also on this flightline as well as Marine Corps EA-6B Prowler electronic warfare aircraft.

A USMC AV-8B Harrier II moves in to take on fuel from an Air Force tanker. Marine Harrier squadrons VMA-311, VMA-331 and VMA-542 participated in DESERT SHIELD/DESERT STORM, and the Marines lost four Harriers in combat and one in a non-combat accident.

An F-14 flies low over the Saudi Desert, armed with the best range of air-to-air weapons carried by any air superiority fighter. These include AIM-54 Phoenix long range missiles, AIM-7 Sparrow medium range missiles, AIM-9 short range missiles and a 20MM Vulcan cannon. The Navy lost one F-14 during DESERT STORM.

A pair of A-7E Corsair IIs of VA-72, off USS JOHN F KENNEDY, refuel from an Air Force KC-135. They are armed with AGM-88A HARM and AIM-9 Sidewinder missiles for a 6 February 1991 SAM hunting mission. (USAF by TSGT Rose Reynolds)

A Jaguar GR.1 of No 6 Squadron, Royal Air Force at RAF Coltishall, at their DESERT SHIELD base at Thumrayt, Oman. Besides the Jaguars, the United Kingdom deployed twenty-four Tornado GR.1 and GR.1A ground attack and reconnaissance aircraft and one squadron (No 11 Squadron) of Tornado F.3 air superiority fighters. In the first three weeks of DESERT STORM, the RAF flew 2,500 of the over 17,000 sorties by coalition air forces, losing six Tornados in combat.

An RAF ground crewman removes the intake cover from a Jaguar prior to a mission. Other RAF aircraft that participated in the war included VC-10K, L-1011 TriStar and Victor tanker aircraft and Nimrods for maritime patrol duty. Jaguars of Nos 41 and 54 Squadrons used 1,000 pound bombs and BL755 CBUs to attack Iraqi airport facilities, Scud launch sites, and Silkworm anti-ship missile sites.

An offshore Kuwaiti pipeline terminal near Kuwait City was set on fire by the Iraqis early in the war. The fire was later extinguished when allied bombers, using smart weapons, destroyed the pumping station which was twelve miles inland. (US Army by SPC William Mol)

Royal Saudi Air Force C-130s and USAF B-52s share the ramp at the giant airfield at King Khalid Military City in Saudi Arabia. One of the success stories of DESERT STORM was the total integration of air assets under a single, unified command. Aircraft from the U.S., United Kingdom, Saudi Arabia, France, United Arab Emirates, Quatar, Kuwait, Bahrain, Oman, Italy and Canada all attacked Iraqi targets under control of U.S., Saudi and NATO AWACS aircraft.

A pair of RSAF Tornados take off on a mission. The Saudi Tornados shared maintenance facilities with British Tornados and both were repaired on a first-come, first-served basis. RSAF flew over 10% of the sorties flown by the coalition, including F-15 CAP missions, Tornado and Hawk interdiction missions, AWACS control missions, and C-130 logistics flights.

A Tornado F-3 of the RSAF, which operates two squadrons of F-3s, No 29 Squadron based at Dhahran and No 34 Squadron based at Tabouk. The Tornado Air Defense Version (ADV) has a maximum takeoff weight of 61,700 pounds, is capable of Mach 2.2 speed and has a ceiling of 70,000 feet. Weapons include an internal cannon and Sky Flash and Sidewinder missiles.

The pilot of a Qatar Emirates Mirage F-1 settles into the cockpit prior to a mission along with F-16s of the 401st TFW. Both aircraft operated from the Qatar base at Doha. Qatar lost no aircraft during DESERT STORM. (USAF by SSGT F. Lee Corkran)

SGT Kim Rinta, Videographer with Det 8, 1365 AVS (based at Hill AFB, Utah) prepares to fly in a United Arab Emirates British-built Hawk strike aircraft. Kim was the first woman to fly backseat in any UAE military jet.

When she returned from the flight, SGT Rinta got the traditional USAF wetting down in congratulation. This was another example of coalition teamwork, cooperation and camaraderie. (USAF by TSGT Marvin Lynchard)

A Kuwaiti A-4KU prepares to take off on a DESERT STORM mission along with a U.S. F-15. The Free Kuwait Air Force flew A-4KU Skyhawks and Mirage F-1s out of their country ahead of the invading Iraqi army. These were fully integrated as a part of the Royal Saudi Air Force. Their only loss was that of the squadron commander, who was shot down and captured on the first day of the war.

An explosive ordnance disposal team assigned to the 4409th Combat Support Group, Eastern Liaison Force 1 Compound, recovers the remains of an Iraqi Scud surface-to-surface missile found 39 kilometers from Riyadh on 21 January 1991. (USAF by SGT Pedro Ybanez)

Coalition Air Force Mirage F-1 fighter pilots pose in front of a Free Kuwait Air Force Mirage F-1. The aircraft was one that escaped from Kuwait and was absorbed into the RSAF, flying missions alongside other Coalition aircraft.

A United Arab Emirates Air Force Mirage 2000 air defense fighter takes off on a combat air patrol mission. The aircraft carries a Matra Magic AAM on the outboard pylon. (USAF by TSGT Perry Heimer)

"THE FACES OF DESERT STORM"

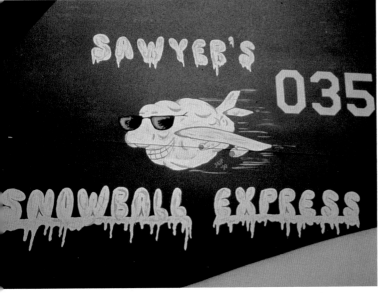